3

For Mr George Smith-Leach.

A wise man once said:

"This is no war of chieftains or of princes, of dynasties or national ambition; it is a war of peoples and of causes. There are vast numbers, not only in this Island but in every land, who will render faithful service in this war, but whose names will never be known, whose deeds will never be recorded. This is a War of the Unknown Warriors".

Winston Churchill, 14th July, 1940.

Thank you for being an Unknown Warrior

Derek

VOICES OF THE BATTLE OF BRITAIN

WRITTEN BY MIKE LEPINE

sona
BOOKS

sona BOOKS

First published 2015 Danann Publishing Ltd / A Flying History Ltd

The publishers would like to thank all the archives for their help in compiling the images for this unique book. All images in this book are copyright and cannot be used or reproduced without the permission of the copyright holders.

Photography courtesy of

Keystone / Getty Images Page 33
Parker / Getty Images Page125
Keith Hamshere / Getty Images Page 113
General Photographic Agency / Getty Images Page 13
Popperfoto / Getty Images Pages 14, 44
Roger Violett / Getty Images Page 22
Jimmy Sime / Getty Images Page 55
Ullstein Bild / Getty Images Pages 9, 27, 29, 36, 59, 65, 73, 77, 82(R), 123
Fox Photos / Getty Images Pages 17(R), 24, 89, 94, 117
Galerie Bildervelt / Getty Images Page 152
Hulton Archive / Getty Images Pages 83, 90
Iwm / Getty Images Pages 51, 106, 108, 116, 127
Central Press / Getty Images Page 31, 133
William Vandivert / The Life Picture Collection / Getty Images Page 110
William Vanderson / Getty Images Jacket, Page 115
Private Collections Pages 5, 17(M), 17(Main), 18, 26, 35, 37-40, 48(Main), 56, 62, 74, 78, 92, 100, 105, 108(R), 109(L), 125, 137, 141
Bae Systems Plc Endpapers, Pages 42, 43, 83, 138,
Wikimedia Commons Pages 11,32, 33, 63, 80, 100, 109(R)
Rolls Royce Plc Pages 46, 47
The Boulton Paul Association Pages 48, 49
Bruce Vigar / Colin Higgs Pages 147(Middle Top), 150(M)
Michael Jowett With Thanks To Aces High Gallery Pages 146 (Top And Centre Bottom), 147(Bottom Centre And Bottom), 148(Top, Top Middle And Bottom). 149(Top And Bottom)
Terry Buck Pages 146(Top Centre And Bottom), 147(Top), 148(Middle Bottom), 149(Middle Top And Bottom)
Jen Gully Page 150(Top)
Tony Pickering Page 151(L)
Terry Clark Pages 145(M) 151(M)
John Ellacombe Pages 145(R) 151(R)
Courtesy Of Group Captain Patrick Tootal Page 145(L)

Book layout & design Darren Grice at **Ctrl-d**

Made in EU.

978-1-912918-20-1
CAT NO: SON0471

CONTENTS

Introduction

In 1997 we completed the production of Battle for the Skies, a seven episode television history of the Royal Air Force. We interviewed more than 20 RAF veterans for the series ranging from a Royal Flying Corps survivor to the joint commander of the British forces in the Gulf War of 1991. Their stories and insight into some vital RAF actions of the past confirmed to us that we should pursue a policy of interviewing as many RAF veterans as possible.

We began a few months later and decided that one key series of interviews we wanted was of those men who flew and fought in the Battle of Britain.

In 2015 there were perhaps 35 surviving veterans of the battle, certainly the most important ever fought in defence of Britain. And the collection of interviews we created is of increasing importance and rarity. Of the 19 unfortunately none are still alive today. Some left the RAF at the end of the war while many of them went on to future distinguished careers in the RAF but it was always the Battle of Britain that stayed vivid in their memories.

Their stories are riveting and insightful yet full of modesty and humour. They talk about not being very good pilots, or just being followers of the aces but underneath it all is a great pride that day after day they flew sortie after sortie against an enemy who had never been beaten until that moment.

They talk of aerial battles perhaps three or four times each day; of the aircraft that carried them into battle without faltering; of the social life in their precious moments of quiet and peace; but most of all they talk about comradeship, friends and colleagues. Some friendships lasted barely a few days while others continue 75 years later.

The 19 who's stories feature in this book are just a few of the almost 3,000 men who flew and fought in that Summer of 1940. Three of them are representative of the men from 15 other countries who joined the RAF to fight. But they also represent the thousands of ground crew, WAAFs, ATA, drivers, plotters, radar operators, airfield defenders, controllers, aircraft builders, cooks, and all the other people without whom the Royal Air Force would have been unable to maintain the fight against Germany.

Colin Higgs & Bruce Vigar

PRELUDE - SEPTEMBER 1939 - JUNE 1940

Prelude to War

As war clouds gathered in Europe during the late 1930s men around Britain and her Empire began to think of the Royal Air Force as a career. For many it was the beginning of a lifelong love of flying

As a young kid I used to go to North Weald aerodrome and see all the Siskins and Bulldogs in the 1920s and 30s, all painted in their squadron colours, gaily painted, and their pilots in their white overalls and they were my heroes. I just thought I'm going to try to do that if they'll have me and that's how it started and as it continued, and I applied for a short service commission in 1938. I was underage, but they said they would accept me, could I go back to school for another term and I said yes, because I wanted to be captain of cricket. They said oh we don't want to interfere with the cricket, old boy, but when you're not playing cricket will you brush up on your maths a little bit. And so that was what happened. I did a term at school, I captained the cricket eleven, I did absolutely nothing at all in the way of work and I went up to Desford in Leicestershire in July of 1939 and in fact war was declared half way through my ab initio training.

Geoffrey Wellum

I wanted to become a fighter pilot and my height was just about right for a fighter pilot and I decided that I would go to Ansty aerodrome, which is only five or six miles from Rugby here, and fly at weekends. We flew on Saturdays and Sundays, Saturday afternoons in actual fact as we worked Saturday mornings. In those days it was a five and a half day week and as an apprentice I had to really get down to work and I had to study at night school three nights a week to get my engineering qualifications.

Tony Pickering

I went up to a place called Ansty which was a civil air set up. They were training RAF pilots ab initio flying so most of the course was these chaps on short service commissions but the VRs were allowed to join this course providing they could get time off from their employer. It was a two month course and Shellmex & BP, for whom I worked in those days, were very generous in that respect. They were very pro service, Shell & BP, so I managed to get eight weeks off, fully paid leave to do my ab initio flying which was very good. There were about half a dozen of us, VRs, on this course and the rest were all short service commissions. Well of course when you joined the VR you automatically became a sergeant, you didn't have a uniform but you were called a sergeant. On my first day at Ansty we were all sitting around in the crew room all togged up in this wonderful flying clothing and a chap came in and said 'Sgt. Foster?' so I said yes and I went forward and he said 'Oh Sgt. Foster, you must have done quite a lot of flying then?' so I said 'I've never been in an aeroplane in my life' and he said 'Oh Christ.' He was a man called Tribe, Pilot Officer Tribe. We didn't get off to a very good start and we never really hit it off.

Bob Foster

I was about ten or eleven years old and we lived in Dunedin. One day three aeroplanes flew over and they looked exciting, so they landed on the mudflats at the end of the road where we lived, the mudflats at Anderson's Bay and my friend and I leapt on our bicycles and charged off down there to see what appeared to be great big aeroplanes. They were Bristol Fighters and out of these aeroplanes came chaps that looked like Gods dressed in white overalls and I thought 'God, look at these fellows here'. That was it and I thought about those aeroplanes for a long time. We moved from Dunedin up to Nelson and about a year or two later, the time when Kingsford-Smith and Ulm were flying round New Zealand in their Fokker three engined job and they came and landed at Nelson. I was one of the first to get out there and got myself ten shillings and we went for a ride in this thing around the Nelson area and I thought 'This is marvellous'. In about 1937 they started the Civil Reserve of Pilots and I thought this was a good chance to learn to fly so I applied and to my delight I was accepted. I was the first boy in Nelson to be accepted and I started towards the end of 1938 in a Gypsy Moth out of the so-called Nelson airfield which actually was a long strip of paddock and I suppose I got maybe two hours, maybe three flights.

John Gard'ner

It was just the fascination of flying which in those days was in its very early years. That would be in the 1920s and 30s. I suppose it was my interest in flying and what every young person at that age, the late teens and early twenties, all they wanted to do was to learn to fly. Just at that time I was stuck in a very boring job working in a bank as a clerk and along came the man from the air ministry who was a recruiting officer from the Air Ministry on a Commonwealth recruiting drive, Australia, New Zealand, Canada, Rhodesia, South Africa and looking for young chaps who could be trained as aircrew for what was known to be then an inevitable war. Providing you were fit and passed a medical, had passed what was called in those days a School Certificate, had the aptitude and ability to enable you to go solo within a very short time, were signing up these young chaps for, or signing up people of that age to take short service commissions in the RAF. The inducement was to take a commission for four years and then two years on the reserve of air force officers and either to be given the option of doing a certain amount of training with the New Zealand Air Force or going direct to England to train with the RAF. Being of a certain temperament I thought this is what I've been waiting for so I signed up in 1938 and at the beginning of 1939 I set sail.

Keith Lawrence

When I was at school in Cape Town one of my friends' brothers was in the Royal Air Force and they were very keen to recruit people, this was in 1938, and it was arranged for us to go and do some flying with a company. We flew in Tiger Moths and they said why don't you come over to England and go to the Air Ministry and we'll see if we can get you into the RAF. So my Dad wasn't very keen about that but we had lots of relatives who lived in England and my Mother was very keen to come over so I came over with her, went to the Air Ministry, had an interview and they said yes we'd like to have you. We'll put you down for a course and as the war was about to break out I joined a group of aircrew who were all Colonials, or Dominions.

John Ellacombe

My first ever flight was at Croydon aerodrome when I was going past with a friend and saw a large notice up advertising flights for five shillings so I thought My God and we both went and had a flight and that was in 1933. I wanted to learn to fly after that but couldn't afford it until 1938 when I saw an advertisement in the local Oxford Mail where I happened to be working at the time. They were asking for volunteers to join the RAF Volunteer Reserve and so I joined on September 1 1938. In those days you were supposed to be under 25 but in fact I was over 25 when I joined. Fortunately they accepted my application just before my birthday in August. I think they would have taken me anyway because at Kidlington they only had 13 pilots when I joined and I was pilot number 13.

William Walker

Ever since I was about that high I always wanted to fly and I think a lot of people in my generation also had the same feeling. Most of us, I have now since found out, had our first flight with Alan Cobham for five shillings and my parents were dead against my ever wanting to fly. I don't know. I think like a lot of parents they thought it was an extremely dangerous pastime. But I went on insisting and eventually after I'd come back from school, I was about 17 or 18 at that time, I picked up a copy of The Aeroplane and in that was an article about a short service commission and it said that once I'd been flying for four years I'd be paid a reasonable amount of money and at the end of four years I would be given a gratuity of £400. I read into gratuity as annuity and I went up to my parents and said 'One of the reasons why flying could be up my street is I'd be paid to do for four years what I want to do and I would be given an annuity of £400", which was a lot of money in those days and they looked at me sideways and said, "That's not an annuity, that's a gratuity and I think that you're so stupid and so backward with your English you can go for an interview but they wouldn't accept you anyway" but they were so hard up that they did accept me.

Billy Drake

British Prime MInister Neville Chamberlain broadcasting the news of the outbreak of war to the nation on 3 September 1939

Life for many in the pre-war Royal Air Force was a gentlemanly affair.

We just flew aeroplanes, We aerobatted aeroplanes and that is about all we ever did. Once a year we went up to an armament practice camp to fire our guns at drogues to see whether we could aim straight and we enjoyed a way of life in those days. The weather was fine and particularly down at Tangmere we had a very nice period where we had the summer routine. We got up very early, did all our flying in the morning and then had the afternoon off and obviously when it was the dark, the evening as well. So it was a gentlemanly existence and our main activity was to fly aeroplanes just for the sake of flying aeroplanes, not to go to war to shoot down this and shoot down that. It was to fly aeroplanes and then to enjoy ourselves with our little cars which we were able to afford. You could then buy a car for five pounds and, if you were very rich you could go up to about ten pounds and that was our existence. War was not paramount at all. What was paramount was to be able to fly that aeroplane that you were involved in.

BILLY DRAKE

Yes we had fun. Mainly in our off duty hours we had fun. The usual thing, in those days anyway, of young men in those circumstances was that we were still fairly disciplined, we had to dress for dinner every night, four nights a week we had to dress in what is known as mess kit and two of the other nights you wore a dinner jacket and the seventh night you could wear a dark lounge suit. You could walk out for your evening meal on Wednesday, Saturday and Sunday, provided you got your CO's permission, and frequently we did do this. We would go to town and have a drink and something to eat and chat among ourselves, enjoy ourselves. We found the evenings fun. You weren't very highly paid so you couldn't go mad but on the other hand things were very much cheaper in 1938. You went out for the evening and if you had five shillings, that's twenty five pence, in your pocket you reckoned you'd be alright. It was autumn / winter 1938.

TERENCE KANE

Whether already in the RAF or just thinking about it, the declaration of war on 3 September 1939 stayed in the memories of all them.

I remember two weeks annual camp, it wasn't RAF Ford then it was a naval station, and we had two weeks each year for training and this was the last two weeks in August 1939. We were in tents and there were signals coming through to the orderly room and people were beginning to talk about war because in the papers it was getting quite serious about the possibility of war and suddenly a signal came through to the orderly room and we had to down canvas immediately. We were taken back by coaches to RAF Kenley, our main station. We were innoculated, given our £5.00 calling up money and told we could go home for a couple of hours, get any extra clothing we wanted and then report back. From there, from Kenley, we were taken down, the squadron moved down to Croydon airport which had then become RAF Croydon and two days later war was declared so I will always remember how that came about.

TERRY CLARK

I remember it very well because being in the VR I got my call-up papers on Friday 1 September, and because I'd trained up at Ansty outside of Coventry and the records had obviously not moved from there, I was told to report to Rugby which was the nearest VR centre, on the Saturday morning. On the Saturday, I'd got a rail warrant, I said farewell to my parents and got the train up to Rugby. They waved me goodbye to go off to war, and I got up to Rugby, went to this centre and the very harassed flying officer said 'Who are you?' and I said 'Sgt. Foster' and he said 'I've never heard of you. I don't know what to do with you. Here's a rail warrant. Go home'. So on the Saturday night, it wa s pouring with rain, I remember that, I came home on leave much to my parents' surprise, and pleasure I suppose. We lived in Battersea in London in those days and so the Sunday 3 September, I remember very well it was a beautiful day, a nice sunny day, at 11 0'clock of course the air raid sirens went off and everyone thought there was going to be a big bombing raid which didn't happen as we know but war was declared and I heard Chamberlain mentioning that we were at war with Germany but I was home on leave then and I stayed there until November when they called me up to carry on with the flying

---

BOB FOSTER

Reid and Sigrist ran the flying school. In those days, diverting a little bit, when they taught you to fly you weren't in the Royal Air Force, you were a civilian pupil pilot and you had to do 50 hours ab initio training and pass that course before they would accept you and, in fact, a good third fell by the wayside, probably a little bit more, but we were sitting in the ante room and we heard this plaintive voice saying that war was declared and it didn't register, not really, you know, nothing changed. The countryside was still the same and then some chap came in who was the director of the flying school. He was rather pompous about attacking the Hun...'We've got a big engine in front of us...', and then someone said well look obviously we, on our little grass airfield in the middle of Leicestershire, our little Tiger Moths, 20 chaps learning to fly are high on the list of priority targets for the Luftwaffe and so obviously we must be a great worry to them so we

are going to be attacked and so they made us taxi all the Tiger Moths and park them round the edge of the airfield, and for this you've got to believe, we were issued with pickaxe handles to defend those aeroplanes to the last man. After two or three days, that was day and night, and of course eventually when the Luftwaffe didn't turn up and the German paratroopers didn't turn up we started flying again. I thought it was silly. As for the war and that very few of us, if any, would get through it, it never occurred to me,

Geoffrey Wellum

I remember very well because on the Friday night, previous to the Sunday when war broke out, they called us all up. We were told by the BBC, that was in those days on the radio, to report to our centres and my centre was at Coventry and I reported to Coventry on the Friday evening. Then they said OK, sign here and go back and on the Sunday we were actually at war but again I sat on my bottom for two weeks before they decided what they were going to do with us. It was something like 20,000 people in the RAFVR, a lot of people and a lot of young men. They couldn't cope with them at first.

Tony Pickering

We knew war was coming and when war was declared as it happened we were out on the airfield, we dispersed our aircraft away from hangars and obvious targets. I made the mistake, when the local civilian air raid warnings went off, I scrambled with my flight because, of course, I didn't want to be caught on the ground as had been happening in Poland and so I got into trouble over that because the station commander said 'I'll tell you when you can fly' and obviously it had to be kept under some sort of control. We had, pre-war, been practicing in sections. We were the first and only squadron to start with to operate with radar and we used to intercept incoming airliners from the continent and pretend we just happened to be in the same piece of airspace as they were at that time. We weren't allowed to approach them closely but we had to report when we first sighted them how far away they were, and what height and so on which was checking on the radar stations who were directing us. We knew it was radar, it was called RDF in those days, Radio Direction Finding, and it was backed up by ground transmitters and receivers. One of us to start off with would have to give a transmission for 30 seconds every three minutes and you had a stopwatch and if you were the detailed squeaker as we called it, when the stopwatch came up you switched on your transmitter on and transmitted for 30 seconds so the ground control stations could get a cross bearing on the plot where you were which was compared with what the radar was saying, how accurate it was and so on which was all great fun and interesting. Officially we weren't allowed to talk about it but apparently, and I didn't know this, I learned after the war, we weren't even supposed to mention it even in our flying logbooks but I used to put it down, RDF exercise. Without it how were you going to intercept incoming aircraft? You'd have to have standing patrols awaiting and then when the raid came in you were probably going to be on the ground refuelling and you hadn't got enough aircraft to keep standing patrols going the whole time so it was vital, in fact we would have been in a very poor situation if we hadn't got radar.

Pete Brothers

When Neville Chamberlain announced that the nation was at last at war with Nazi Germany, at 11.15am on Sunday, 3 September 1939, it was widely anticipated that the Battle of Britain would begin within a matter of hours. It would be short, brutal and most probably apocalyptic. Military theory had become conflated with the science fiction of H. G. Wells, Olaf Stapledon and Nevil Shute. It was anticipated that vast and seemingly unending bomber fleets would come out of the east, blackening the skies and swatting impotent little fighter aircraft aside like flies. Whole cities would be reduced to rubble in minutes, the survivors choking and dying in the thick clouds of poison gas clinging to the ruins. Cholera, typhoid and dysentery would claim those meagre few who yet remained. Civilisation would collapse and anarchy hold sway. Looking back, Harold Macmillan said that he and others in high places *'thought of air warfare in 1938 rather as people think of nuclear war today'.* Even one of the most influential military thinkers of the time, Basil Liddell Hart, predicted there might be a quarter of a million civilian casualties within just a week.

Just before 11.30am, the air raid sirens sounded, setting off every dog within earshot and worrying the horses. People looked up. One person, it is reported, died of fright. And then, eventually, the all-clear sounded. If the Luftwaffe was coming, it wouldn't be today.

To the east, in Berlin, Adolf Hitler was genuinely shocked when Great Britain and France declared war on him. He had assumed that their protestations over the Nazi invasion of Poland were just another bluff and that they would continue to do everything they could to appease him as they had done in the past. Now he was at war with the most powerful land army in Europe and the greatest navy in the world – and for a moment he panicked. Stalking around his office

while furiously consuming box after box of pralines (He called them his *'nerve medicine'*), the Fuhrer stared at his senior Commanders and asked them, *'now what?'*

Hitler too thought that the world was about to come crashing in on him. At any moment he might receive reports of the French Army invading the Fatherland from the south, or the Royal Navy sailing to blockade his ports. Perhaps the Armée de l'Air and the RAF would formate and roll across his cities, pounding them to dust. Hitler's panic lasted for several days, but when nothing continued to happen and it became increasingly obvious that the French and British didn't know what to do either, his fear turned to fury.

Hitler swiftly became obsessed with drawing up grandiose attack plans with all the strategic genius that had, during his military career, propelled him to the stratospheric heights of corporal. His forces were not ready to launch an offensive against the west and the winter of 1939 was the worst for many years. Neither fact troubled him. His commanders meanwhile used every skill at their disposal to keep him from doing anything until at least the spring of 1940 when they would be adequately prepared.

The job of drawing up a plan of attack for Spring 1940 fell to General Franz Halder, Chief of the General Staff of the Army Supreme Command and the architect of the invasion of Poland. When Halder wasn't trying to work out how to beat the superior French Army, he was trying to figure out how to kill Hitler. He considered just going in and shooting him. He considered explosives. He considered a conspiracy – but in the end his nerve just deserted him. He put his head down and did his job like a good soldier.

And so for eight months nothing much happened. The British called it *'The Phoney War'*. The Germans, in a display of wit, called it *'The Sitzkrieg'*. And through it all Hitler seethed and was wracked by nerves in turn. He hated the French. He had nothing but contempt for them. Partly it was Germany's humiliation at Versailles after the Great War that fuelled his hate. Partially it was the old German animosity towards its traditional enemy. Partially it was what he perceived as a Gallic attitude of casual arrogance. He would enjoy seeing France burn when the weather permitted. Britain however was different. The Fuhrer quite liked and admired Britain. He liked its history and heritage, felt some sort of genetic near-kinship with (most of) its people and thought that the British Empire was a thing of splendour. He didn't really want to go to war with Britain – and so he made a self-pleasing assumption that he wouldn't have to. Instead, once he crushed France, he convinced himself that the dull, grey cowards running Britain (an opinion he formed during the Munich crisis) would simply roll over and almost beg him for a settlement. He would be generous, he fantasised. He would have Europe. Britain could have the rest of the world – as long as it answered to him.

Through the 'Sitzkrieg', like the good soldiers they were, Hitler's Commanders looked at some potential invasion plans should it become necessary to force a military settlement on Britain. The Kriegsmarine began first in November 1939, identifying the need to eliminate both the Royal Air Force and the Royal Navy before any landings could be made. The Wehrmacht followed with their own plans, suggesting an attack from the Low Countries against England's east coast from the Wash to the Thames Estuary. Reichsmarschall Hermann Goering, head of the Luftwaffe and Hitler's Deputy, was contemptuous of both plans. Britain, he said, would need to be comprehensively defeated first. Through it all, Hitler remained curiously detached from it all and dreamed on of a negotiated peace with Britain. Any thought of a seaborne assault against England sent him rushing for the pralines again. *'At sea I am a coward,'* he confessed.

At dawn on 10 May 1940, Hitler finally unleashed what he called *'Operation Yellow'*. History would come to know it as 'The Blitzkrieg'. Two armoured corps and paratrooper units, with close air support provided by the Luftwaffe, burst into Belgium and the Netherlands, fighting south towards France.

That very same day, by complete coincidence, everything changed in Great Britain. Neville Chamberlain's government fell and Winston Churchill became Prime Minister. Churchill was not even a popular choice for the position, but arch-appeaser Lord Halifax had turned down the role and Chamberlain decided not to fight for his own job. Those who favoured peace with Germany at any price were seriously perturbed by what Churchill might do once he got his hands on the reins of power, being a notorious opponent of appeasement. Many of his colleagues in the Conservative Party genuinely disliked him and had conspired to wreck his career over the past decade or so. Others considered him a has-been. He was 65 and a back-bencher, after all. Hitler, who barely thought about Churchill, wrote him off as a drunk and a Jew-lover. He didn't know it, but *'cometh the hour…'*.

Churchill's first few weeks as Prime Minister during May and June 1940 turned into, quite literally, a baptism of fire. In response to the German Blitzkrieg, French forces - along with significant elements of the British Expeditionary Force stationed in France - moved forward into Belgium to confront the invading army head on. It was a trap. To their east, a mass of German armour poured out of the supposedly

Ground crew race to prepare Hawker Hurricanes for take off

impassable Ardennes Forest and swiftly powered their way westward to the sea. The Allies were cut off and surrounded.

The RAF had been in action, with mixed results, since the first day of the Blitzkrieg. Operating from airfields in France, RAF Hurricane fighters had acquitted themselves well fighting alongside the French Air Force and other allies. The end of the first day's fighting saw 61 RAF aircraft lost or damaged to the Luftwaffe's 192. The light British bombers on the other hand proved disastrously ineffectual and vulnerable. Thirty-two Fairey Battles were sent against the Germans. Of those, thirteen were swiftly shot down and another 18 severely damaged. Of a flight of Blenheims from 600 Squadron sent out on patrol, only one survived. Five Battles were sent out to destroy important bridges at Maastricht on the 12 May. None returned. Two days later, the Battle Fleet set out to bomb again. Seventy one took off. Thirty one returned. Air Officer Commanding-in-Chief British Air Forces in France, Air Marshal Barratt, is said to have openly wept when he saw the casualty figures.

Just six days into the blitzkrieg, the French Prime Minister Paul Reynaud rang Winston Churchill and told him it was all over. *'We have been defeated,'* he said. *'We are beaten. We have lost the battle.'* The Netherlands surrendered that same day. Churchill was a Francophile and found it hard to accept that the French would collapse so easily and so abjectly. He wanted everyone to fight on and was willing to pump more and more resources into the battle, including precious RAF fighter squadrons.

This alarmed Air Chief Marshal Sir Hugh Dowding, Air Officer Commanding RAF Fighter Command. He had always seen his role as defending Britain's shores rather than fighting foreign battles and swiftly made his views known. The RAF had now lost 250 Hurricane fighters over France in the few days between 8 and 18 May and such losses were simply unsustainable. To feed more aircraft into the maelstrom could leave the British Isles defenceless in the event of an invasion. Dowding was summoned to the War Cabinet Room on 15 May and told that his reluctance to commit aircraft to France endangered Britain's relations with France and also hampered the defence of British troops. Dowding stood his ground. He said *' I am well aware of the situation Prime Minister, but my task at hand is for the air defence of this country and it is my belief that I cannot achieve this if half my aircraft are in France'.* He then provided Churchill with a detailed report on Hurricane losses – and the growing shortage of pilots. *'This red line shows the wastage of Hurricanes in the last few days. If the line goes on at the same rate for the next 10 days, there won't be a single Hurricane left in either France*

LEFT & TOP: The Dornier Do17, sometimes nicknamed 'The Flying Pencil', was one of the three main bombers used by the Luftwaffe in their Blitzkrieg. As a bomber against strategic targets it had its limitations **MIDDLE:** Hurricanes of 111 Squadron fly in formation from their Northolt base in May 1940; **RIGHT:** The Front Line! A Hurricane pilot, in his cockpit and ready for take off at Hawkinge, the nearest airfield on the British mainland to occupied France

The only thing you really saw was this phenomenal plume of black smoke over Dunkirk so I don't think we could have done any more than we did. The main thing is that we were so few. When you remember how far we had to fly, because of our endurance, we didn't have long range tanks, we could only have perhaps an hour, perhaps less, over there and to try and keep that up in May which is sunshine from half past five until ten or eleven at night how could we be there all the time. And we took casualties. Some squadrons were shot out of the sky. Although we shot down many more Germans than casualties on our side so we think, we were down to nine aircraft on the second day and those have to be replaced pretty quickly, with pilots untrained, so we were given a couple of days off and back in the fray again. It was more intense from my point of view than the Battle of Britain.

ALLAN WRIGHT, 92 SQUADRON

or England!'

It was not something Churchill wanted to hear - and he almost tried to turn a deaf ear to it by deliberately getting some statistics ' muddled up' but, as he flew in and out of France to consult with the increasingly chaotic French government, it rapidly dawned on him that France was indeed finished and he would be better off conserving his fighters to defend Britain as Dowding wanted. The French were furious and felt betrayed – but could do nothing.

By 24 May, German panzers had reached the Channel ports and Britain was looking to evacuate and rescue what it could of its troops marooned in Belgium. The answer they came up with was Operation Dynamo, to concentrate their forces on the port of Dunkirk and then to send small boats into the shallows to pluck soldiers from the waters and take them out to where RN destroyers and other big ships were waiting. They hoped that, at most, they might rescue as many as 40,000 men.

On 26 May, the Allied evacuation at Dunkirk began. Looking on, Goering chuckled and said *'I hope the Tommies are good swimmers!'* Back in England, the fighters of 11 Group under Air Vice Marshal Keith Park were tasked with flying across the Channel and providing air cover. Flying in support of Operation Dynamo, 11 Group lost 106 fighters and sixty pilots including three squadron commanders. However, the men waiting helplessly on the beaches below had no real idea of the RAF's efforts. All they could hear was the screams of Stuka dive bombers overhead. Thick, low cloud masked the desperate dogfights going on above their heads – and Park's policy of trying to intercept German bombers before they arrived over the beaches meant that significant numbers of engagements were too far away to be witnessed. As a result, many troops thought they were receiving no air cover and returned to England hating the RAF.

Dynamo finally came to an end on 3 June 1940. During the evacuation, Fighter Command had flown over 2,700 combat sorties and the evacuation had been an incredible success - 224,686 British and 121,445 French and Belgian troops had been exhausted, dispirited, defeated. They had left most of their kit behind, including their rifles and machine guns. The beaches were littered with abandoned supplies, vehicles, ammunition and artillery pieces. The army that returned home to Britain had next to nothing with which to fight off an invasion, should it come.

The first week of June saw the Luftwaffe launch a number of small scale bombing raids on east and south east England. The purpose of the raids was to give Luftwaffe crews some experience of what was to come – should it be necessary. On 10 June, when it was quite safe to do so, Italy entered the war. On 12 June, the Wehrmacht marched into Paris. On 18 June, the last Hurricane squadrons left France to return home for the battle to come, simply abandoning 120 damaged or otherwise unserviceable Hurricanes on their bases. Of the 452 fighter aircraft the RAF had based in France, only 66 returned safely. The battle for France had cost the RAF a total of 1,029 aircraft – aircraft that they could barely afford to lose. However, the Luftwaffe had suffered significant casualties too. They had lost 1,428 aircraft with approximately another 500 seriously damaged.

On 22 June, France officially surrendered to Germany. The war in Europe was over. Now Britain braced for what was surely to follow and the Germans worked furiously to consolidate their gains. Luftwaffe forces rushed to occupy new captured forward air bases in Northern France and Belgium, and to replenish the losses sustained during the Blitzkrieg. In England, Dowding tried to consolidate his forces and co-ordinate his defences. Britain mobilised at an astonishing speed with over 500,000 men putting on uniform. Few though had guns to go with their khakis.

General Erhard Milch, State Secretary for the German Air Ministry, now argued that there was absolutely no time to lose and that German paratroopers should be dropped at the earliest possible moment on strategic sites in south east England. Once dug in, they would hold their ground until an invasion force could relieve them. Goering described Milch's ideas as *'nonsense'*. He hated Milch.

Hitler was in an even stranger than usual state of mind. He had won the Blitzkrieg in record time and was thoroughly enjoying humiliating the French but when it came to committing to the invasion of Britain, he flinched. For some reason, the thought of a seaborne invasion chilled him. It was a phobia he shared – quite ironically - with Churchill, (who had been traumatised by the ill-fated Gallipoli landings for which he had been partially responsible during the Great War). Instead, Hitler still thought he could reason with Britain. *'I'll come to an understanding with England,'* he had told Goering on 18 June. To von Rundstedt he said, *'I will make peace with England and offer her an alliance'*. He was already in secret talks with both the IRA and Welsh Nationalists about a post-settlement Britain. He just hadn't got the measure of Winston Churchill yet.

Certain members of Churchill's War Cabinet had been more than amenable to any chance of peace with Germany ever since they had first met. Chamberlain thought a *'compromise'* should be sought while Lord Halifax had secretly been discussing peace terms with the

A Spitfire Mk I patrols the coast

Italian Ambassador. Churchill was of a different mind. *'My policy,'* he declared, *'is a policy of war.'* On 28 May, he had told his cabinet, *'If this long island story of ours is to end at last, let it end only when each one of us lies choking in his own blood upon the ground'.*

If Hitler wanted Britain, he'd have to fight for her.

Neither the German navy nor the army were particularly enamoured of launching a seaborne invasion. The Kriegsmarine had taken a ferocious mauling during the Norwegian Campaign back in April and the Wehrmacht were staggered by the logistical implications and nervous of their own inexperience. Neither service had any real idea as to how to achieve an invasion. Certain army elements thought crossing the Channel would be just like crossing a very big river. The Kriegsmarine assured them it would not be like that at all. It was Goering in his capacity as head of the Luftwaffe who – as usual – knew just what the Fuhrer wanted to hear from him. Relishing the chance to embarrass the rival armed forces, he told Hitler he had absolute confidence in his air force's ability to blow the RAF from the skies. It would take about four weeks, he boasted and – when it was complete – the British would sue for peace knowing they were defenceless. There might never be the need to launch an invasion. Goering's confidence was infectious. Hitler was sold. By mid-June, the Kriegsmarine had got hold of 45 inland barges and busied themselves experimenting with them – just in case.

Back in May 1940, an American journalist sat down to interview Air Vice Marshal Charles Blount who had commanded the RAF squadrons in France. He asked Blount, *'What's going to happen when the French are beaten and the Germans can turn their whole air force on to this country?'*

Blount looked him and said *'They're going to get the shock of their lives'.*

Battle of France

The Battle of France and the evacuation from Dunkirk took just a few short weeks but the experiences of the RAF against the experienced Luftwaffe pilots helped enormously to prepare them and the rest of the RAF pilots for what was ahead over Britain. Four pilots tell their experiences of those days in May and June 1940

We still considered ourselves to be as good as anyone else, as good as any of the 109 pilots we would meet, which we didn't very often, and that we could look after ourselves. 1 Squadron was posted out to France so we lived a different type of life in France to our opposite numbers who stayed back in England and again we had nobody to talk to about war. The French just sat back and had some very good lunches and very good dinners but we very rarely saw them. We had no radar and the only operational activities were when we saw contrails above us and we realised, probably, that it would be a German aeroplane going back to Germany.

Billy Drake

It had been very quiet and we weren't given any information at all. We realised something was happening at three o'clock in the morning when we heard aeroplanes flying all over the place. We said well that can't be the RAF and then when daylight came up we realised the Germans had started. As a result of that we moved from Vasincourt to another base closer to Rheims.

Billy Drake

You were sometimes called to readiness to man your aircraft for no apparent reason and told you had to sleep in the dispersal hut, that sort of thing, and so it was a great relief and you could then say now we can get organised and we know what we're doing. The Battle of France was going on and our sister squadron from Biggin Hill was moved to France and, late on, after 10 May when the German advance was so rapid, we were sent out to reinforce in France. We would fly out at first light, leave Biggin Hill in the dark, fly to France, land where we'd been told to land at some little airfield, refuel which we had to do ourselves from tins because we had no ground crew with us, and then we would operate but it became chaos. We couldn't get any orders or instructions because the headquarters was constantly on the move, retreating, and food, nothing had been arranged. One of our pilots was fluent in French and I remember he managed to beg some bread from a farmhouse near the airfield which was all we got that day and we would fly back as it was getting dark, land back at Biggin Hill just about in the dark. By that time, of course, you'd been up since four o'clock in the morning and you got back about ten o'clock at night, have a meal, go to bed, be shaken awake again about half past three, get up, get washed and shaved, down to have a quick snack breakfast and off onto the airfield and take off for France. That was very tedious, very tiring and we didn't feel we were making any great contribution because we only had the odd engagement. We were on a French airfield one day and a French fighter aircraft was doing aerobatics over the airfield. A German bomber, a Dornier 17, steamed over the airfield at about 2,000 feet and we thought he was going to come back, bomb us and catch us all on the ground. Fortunately he had a plan and he was going somewhere else and we said to the French base commander who was standing nearby 'Look, a German aircraft and you have an aircraft doing aerobatics. Tell him, he's obviously not seen the German' and the French commander said 'Today he is only authorised for aerobatics and not combat' and so we thought 'That's a great help. We look forward to the help of the French air force, thank you very much.'

PETE BROTHERS

We were moving from base to base, moving from billet to billet and if we weren't doing that we were standing by and if we weren't standing by we were in the bloody air and being told where to go. My first real recollection of actual warfare was my last trip of that period when I went up in a section of four aeroplanes with Prosser Hanks leading and I was not in my own aeroplane but in another one. I got to 18,000 feet and I realised I had no oxygen so I called up the leader and said 'I have no oxygen, instructions please.' In a very curt way he told me to bugger off home which I was in the process of doing when I saw three Dorniers. I don't think they saw me because I got behind one quite close and was able to inflict enough damage to realise I'd shot something down. I was in the process of getting behind the leader when I found somebody had got behind me and I hadn't seen them. I had broken all the rules I'd been teaching myself over the last four years, not looking behind, and this was a Messerschmitt 110 and he got me good and proper. I was flaming, covered in glycol, covered in everything you could think of and panicking to get out of the aeroplane. I undid everything and then realised as I banged my head that I hadn't released the hood which probably saved my life because the flames were coming up and had I opened the hood, I was covered in petrol anyway, the flames would have got me. By the time I decided the hood should be released I was upside down so fell out. I had been hit

British destroyers, with RAF escort, head back to Britain crammed with troops picked up from the Dunkirk beaches *with bullets in my back and legs and I thought, at one period, that my leg had been shot off. Bits of shrapnel had hit me but when I landed with my parachute I realised that perhaps I had two legs still and then I came across the next nasty shock. A lot of French farmers with scythes and all sorts of instruments were coming up towards me and they were absolutely certain I was a German. I found it very difficult to be able to show them my RAF wings but by the time they got close enough to be really lethal I was able to demonstrate and tell them that I was an English pilot and they couldn't have been kinder so they got me to a French unit, medical unit, and I was met there by two French orderlies who said in their very best French that they were very sorry but the doctors weren't available becaus they had gone home for lunch and in any case there was no anasthetic. I was to grit my teeth while they got hold of all the stuff out of my back. I appreciated what outlaws and other people in America must have felt when they were being medically looked after without any anasthetic.*

Billy Drake

It was awful, there's no other way to put it. You suddenly found yourself up against enormous odds. I'll give you one example, six of us ran into 40 Ju87s one day. We shot down 14 of them and they ran off. As we left, and we were out of ammunition another 150 Ju87s came in. We were never overawed by the Germans but we were certainly outnumbered. We quickly learned the German tactics were good and we'd been taught to fly World War 1 tactics, tight formations, vics, to show that we were well disciplined in the air I suppose as much as anything but in actual fact it was a recipe for disaster. We could have been killed, and we were, picked off. The Germans used to pick us off one by one. We weren't looking behind us, so quickly we learned the Germans' way of weaving so then we could always keep looking behind us. We learned to take our collars and ties off. We used to wear the tight Van Heusen collar, which incidentally killed a lot of people. When they went in the sea the collar tightened up so we learned that trick to take them off. Also, by taking the collar off, you could turn your neck more.

Dennis David

We were sent over Dunkirk, we weren't even told at that time why we were sent over Dunkirk, we were just told to fly up and down not below 10,000 feet, and if we came across the enemy shoot him down. So we got there and we started patrolling and I was interested in the situation in the countryside round Dunkirk. The first thing I was aware of was seeing several silver coloured aeroplanes passing by a little below and thinking what a pretty sight but it was only then that someone said '109s!' and I realised we needed to do something about it. Somehow I hadn't just switched on to a wartime situation. Well I hadn't met the enemy before.

Allan Wright

Dunkirk was an absolute eye opener. A smoking city covered almost in a pall of smoke. It brought home to me that war was not going to be all that funny. There was the Odeon cinema in Calais burning nicely, you thought that could be our local Odeon in Bromley. This is not good enough. I don't like this and it's very serious. We didn't hang about over Dunkirk. We tried to get inland a bit to intercept aircraft before they got to Dunkirk. There was no point in sitting over the target and catching the chap just as he was dropping his bombs, that was too late. You wanted to get in before that so you were trying to operate about ten miles further inland from Dunkirk itself but it was quite a shattering experience to see what was taking place.

Pete Brothers

For some reason during the lull that occurred whilst the Germans were obviously getting reorganised we moved to Hawkinge every day and we then did a 'fly the flag' operation down the French coast to Rouen and back again. Apparently the idea was to show the Germans we were still in existence despite having cleared out of France and it was pointless. In fact it was jolly dangerous and we lost people because the Germans would just have another cup of coffee when they saw us flying out and down the coast and by the time we had turned round for home at Rouen and set off back, of course the sun was behind us which was no way to get mixed up with the enemy. The Germans took off, climbed up into the sun and got behind us where we couldn't see them and then they'd start picking us off and we lost several chaps that way. After a few days of this fortunately the AOC Air Vice Marshal Park arrived in his Hurricane to see how we were getting on and I'm afraid I was a bit short tempered because I was tired and because I was frightened and told him what I thought of this ridiculous operation and the next day we were not called on to do it again which was a great relief.

Pete Brothers

'We Shall Fight Them on the Beaches...'

On 4 June , Winston Churchill told the nation:

'Even though large tracts of Europe and many old and famous States have fallen or may fall into the grip of the Gestapo and all the odious apparatus of Nazi rule, we shall not flag or fail. We shall go on to the end. We shall fight in France, we shall fight on the seas and oceans, we shall fight with growing confidence and growing strength in the air, we shall defend our island, whatever the cost may be. We shall fight on the beaches, we shall fight on the landing grounds, we shall fight in the fields and in the streets, we shall fight in the hills; we shall never surrender.'

After making the speech, Churchill confided in a friend,

'And we'll fight them with the butt ends of broken beer bottles because that's bloody well all we've got...' .

The 'Finest Hour' Speech

On 18 June , Churchill made his famous 'Finest Hour' speech before a packed House of Commons. In it he gave a name to the battle to come. He called it 'the Battle of Britain'.

'...the Battle of Britain is about to begin. Upon this battle depends the survival of Christian civilisation. Upon it depends our own British life, and the long continuity of our institutions and our Empire. The whole fury and might of the enemy must very soon be turned on us. Hitler knows that he will have to break us in this island or lose the war. If we can stand up to him, all Europe may be freed and the life of the world may move forward into broad, sunlit uplands. But if we fail, then the whole world, including the United States, including all that we have known and cared for, will sink into the abyss of a new dark age made more sinister, and perhaps more protracted, by the lights of perverted science. Let us therefore brace ourselves to our duties, and so bear ourselves, that if the British Empire and its Commonwealth last for a thousand years, men will still say, this was their finest hour.'

Sir Winston Churchill, honorary commodore of 615 Squadron, inspects the parade. 615 flew Hurricanes during the early part of the Battle of Britain

Squaring Up to the Enemy

Hermann Goering in 1932

Adolf Hitler, Hermann Goering, Joseph Goebbels & Rudolf Hess at Nazi Party Rally

Reichsmarschall Hermann Goering

'Born of the spirit of the German airmen in the First World War, inspired by the faith in our Fuhrer and Commander-in-Chief thus stands the German Air Force today, ready to carry out every command of the Fuhrer with lightning speed and undreamed-of might.'

GOERING

Hermann Goering was not just the head of the Luftwaffe. He was also Hitler's designated deputy – which made him the second most powerful man in Nazi Germany – and something of a national celebrity. During the First World War, he had achieved fame as a well decorated fighter ace with the fledgling German Air Force. By war's end he had been promoted to the head of Baron von Richthofen's legendary Flying Circus and had 22 confirmed kills to his credit.

Goering was an early and enthusiastic Nazi, joining the party in 1922 after hearing Hitler give a speech. *'It was political love at first sight,'* he later confessed. He had to flee the country a year later after the Munich Beer-Hall putsch, when he was shot in the groin. During his exile he spent time in two lunatic asylums - one for particularly dangerous patients where he was made to wear a straightjacket – bloated up to 280 lbs and developed his first taste for serious opiate abuse to alleviate the sometimes excruciating pain in his crotch. He was granted amnesty and returned home to Germany in 1927.

When Hitler was appointed Chancellor in 1933, Goering was given a number of important posts while also distinguishing himself by suggesting the Nazis adopt the Swastika emblem, establishing the Gestapo and the SS and becoming deeply involved in the early planning of the Holocaust. He became Commander-in-Chief of the Luftwaffe on 1 March 1935 and designed his own unique powder blue uniform for the post which came complete with a jewel-encrusted baton.

In private, Goering was a paranoid who never made friends with other members of the Nazi elite whom he felt were always trying to weaken his influence with Hitler. He lived in a palace in Berlin where he threw decadent parties, took drugs for the recurring pain in his wounded groin and dined to excess – a lifestyle funded mostly by vigorous bribe-taking. He loved to dress up in exotic costumes and flamboyant jewellery that eventually sparked rumours of secret transvestitism. However, he was popular with ordinary Germans, who ironically saw him as *'manly'*. His palace – and his other properties – were increasingly decorated with looted art treasures (By war's end it was estimated he had a collection worth $200 million)

Goering also owned one of the world's largest toy train sets, which he allowed visiting Luftwaffe commanders to play with as well as his own personal real life train, codenamed Asia. It was on this train that he would move around during the Battle of Britain. It was protected by its

Albert Kesselring

Albert Kesselring with Luftwaffe officers

own anti-aircraft guns, had luxury toilet suites and two entire wagons that were always kept empty in case Goering felt like going shopping – or looting. When not in use, it was always kept in sidings close to a tunnel – just in case of an air raid.

Generalfeldmarschall Albert Kesselring

Kesselring was one of the most popular and respected German Commanders of the Second World War. His men loved him and referred to him as *'Uncle'*. The British called him *'Smiling Albert'*. Kesselring had originally trained for the highly precarious post of balloon observer for the artillery before the First World War and served with distinction on both the Western and Eastern fronts during that war.

Against his wishes, he was let go by the German army in 1933 and instead transferred to the forerunner of the German Air Ministry that same year, helping to build a fledgling Luftwaffe. He became Chief of Staff of the Luftwaffe in 1936 and, in October 1938, was given command of Luftflotte I with the rank of Air General.

Luftflotte I provided close air support to Army Group North during the invasion of Poland in 1939 and Kesselring was personally shot down by the Polish Air Force during operations, but survived. He would go on to be shot down four more times during the war. He was transferred to command of Luftflotte II in January 1940. Luftflotte II went on to provide close air support during the Blitzkrieg in May 1940 and Kesselring's success as commander saw him promoted to Generalfeldmarschall. Luftflotte II was then committed to the Battle of Britain from bases in France and Belgium.

Generalfeldmarschall Hugo Sperrle

Sperrle was the commanding officer of Luftflotte III during the Battle of Britain and – according to Adolf Hitler himself – *' one of my two most brutal-looking generals'*. Hitler liked to take Sperrle with him on the occasional foreign visit, just to intimidate the local politicians. Sperrle enjoyed the high life, awarding himself luxury accommodation in Paris after the fall of France and was prone to bellowing *'don't you know who I am?'* when not given the very best table in a restaurant.

Like his superior Goering, Sperrle had served with distinction in the air during World War One, enjoying rapid promotion from aircraft observer to commander of the air components of the German 7th Army by war's end. Sperrle joined the Luftwaffe as soon as it was formed and served as the first commander of the notorious Kondor Legion during the Spanish Civil War. The outbreak of World War Two saw him promoted and in charge of Luftflotte III, which took no part in the invasion of Poland but which played a major role in the Blitzkrieg of May 1940, where it provided close air support to the Wehrmacht as it fought through the low countries and Northern France. He was promoted to Generalfeldmarschall in July 1940, in preparation for commanding Luftflotte III during the Battle of Britain.

Generaloberst Hans-Jürgen Stumpff

Stumpff served as an officer with the German Army in the First World War. After Hitler came to power, he transferred to the new Luftwaffe and served as Chief of General Staff from June 1937 to January 1939. In early 1940 he took command of Luftflotte I before assuming responsibility for the new Luftflotte V which was located in occupied Norway and Denmark. Luftflotte V was considerably smaller than Luftflotte I and II.

Stumpff faced a particularly difficult responsibility during the Battle of Britain. Because of the long distance his aircraft would have to fly, his bombers couldn't rely on any significant fighter cover because of fuel considerations. German Intelligence believed that RAF Fighter Command would have to send any Hurricanes and Spitfires defending the East Coast and Scotland down to shore up the defences of southern England and so the lack of fighter cover wouldn't matter. The bombers of Luftflotte V would see no resistance. In practice, things would turn out very differently.

Hans-Jürgen Stumpf (right) shaking hands with Finnish general, Hjalmar Siilasvuo

Kesselring, Sperrle, Hitler, Goering and Milch pose for an official photograph

Air Chief Marshal Sir Hugh Dowding

Air Chief Marshal Sir Hugh Dowding accompanying King George VI and Queen Elizabeth during a visit to Bentley Priory

Air Chief Marshal Sir Hugh Dowding Air Officer Commanding RAF Fighter Command

Sir Hugh Dowding became the most important commander during the Battle of Britain simply because everybody who mattered hated him.

Born in Scotland in 1882, Hugh Dowding trained for an army life and from 1900 onward wandered the Empire with the Garrison Artillery but then became intrigued by early aviation. He was awarded Aviator's Certificate no. 711 in 1913 after attending the Vickers School of Flying at Brooklands and won his wings at the Central Flying School.

He served as a flier throughout the First World War, rising to the rank of temporary Brigadier-General by 1917. The post-war era saw him in a variety of roles with the newly established RAF, including Head of Research and Development. In December 1929, Dowding became Air Officer Commanding Fighting Area, Air Defence of Great Britain. He was promoted to Air Marshal in 1933 and became CO of RAF Fighter Command in 1936 – which was seen as a quite deliberate snub to the man.

Dowding was not considered either a *'good egg'* or a *'spiffing fellow'* by his fellow officers in the RAF or the men from the Air Ministry. In his younger days he had been an international slalom skiing champion but since the tragic death of his wife after only two years of marriage, he had become something of a recluse, bringing up his infant son in private with the help of his sister. He didn't go to parties. He didn't stroke the right personalities. He didn't play politics. He didn't join the right clubs. His fellow officers called him *'stuffy'*. Even his old wartime CO, the head of the RFC, Sir Hugh Trenchard, called him *'a dismal Jimmy'* behind his back and did the best he could to wreck his career. (Trenchard would later be stunned by Dowding's achievement in winning the Battle of Britain and apologised).

And so it was that Dowding ended up in charge of the post no-one wanted – Head of Fighter Command. The Air Ministry at the time believed the maxim that *'the bomber will always get through'* (as Stanley Baldwin had said in 1932) and that any air war would be decided by who had the largest and most powerful bomber fleet. Fighters were seen as insignificant and inconsequential. It was quite typical then that, when Dowding turned up quietly one morning in 1936 at his new HQ at RAF Bentley Priory in Stanmore with no entourage and no fuss, that no-one believed who he was and that he was very nearly refused entry and turned away. He was now 54, a widower living nearby to the base with his sister.

Largely ignored and shunned, Dowding had nevertheless had a powerful – indeed vital – effect on the RAF. He championed radar (then called RDF). He fought for the development of advanced monoplane fighters – first the Hurricane and then the Spitfire – even when the Air Ministry wanted to devote their budget to bombers. He also developed what became known as the Dowding System, a way of integrating radar, ground observers, communication links and fighter aircraft all working efficiently together as a screen against bombers.

Dowding achieved all this – and more – despite being at a huge disadvantage. Regardless of his personality and popularity, the Air Ministry was essentially planning for peace while Nazi Germany was building for war. Eager to enjoy a *'peace dividend'*, the British government deeply resented money spent on defence. Dowding was convinced RAF fighter bases needed concrete all weather runways. The ministry refused to countenance such a profligate waste of money. They even told him that they could not afford the cost of installing bulletproof glass in his Hurricanes. Dowding retorted, *'If Chicago gangsters can ride behind bulletproof glass, I see no reason why my pilots should not do so too.'* This time he got his way.

In 1937, Dowding was promoted to Air Chief Marshal. He was all set to retire in 1939 (with the enthusiastic support of the Air Ministry), but was asked to stay on because of the worsening international situation. During the Blitzkrieg, Dowding unfortunately added Churchill to his long list of enemies by fighting so vigorously to retain the bulk of RAF fighters for home defence purposes instead of squandering them over France. Throughout this time, Dowding was given virtually no idea whether he would be kept on in his job. In early July 1940, he was still expecting to be forcibly retired at any moment and was only - grudgingly – asked to stay on until October 1940 – in a letter received 5 July – five days before the Battle of Britain officially began.

As the Battle of Britain loomed, Dowding seemed a very remote figure to the pilots under his command. Most of them didn't even know what he looked like. He never visited their airfields. Some thought it was aloofness or arrogance. They couldn't have been more wrong. In reality, Dowding was chronically shy and thought that turning up at the RAF stations would just prove a silly and frivolous distraction. In private, he couldn't have cared more for the men he referred to as *'my chicks'* – and his now-adult son Derek would be quietly fighting alongside them as one of **'The Few'.**

Air Chief Marshal Sir Hugh Dowding and an aide with several Battle of Britain fighter pilots, representing "The Few" outside the Air Ministry in London during the celebration of the second anniversary of the RAF's most successful day of the Battle

Keith Park, an Air Vice Marshal in 1940, seen here as Air Marshal later in the war

Air Vice Marshal Trafford Leigh-Mallory

Air Vice Marshal Keith Park

'If ever any one man won the Battle of Britain, he (Park) did. I don't believe it is realised how much that one man, with his leadership, his calm judgment and his skill, did to save not only this country, but the world'

Lord Tedder

A New Zealander by birth (from a Scots family), Park first saw action at Gallipoli in 1915 as an NCO in the artillery. After transferring to the British Royal Horse and Field Artillery, he was injured during the Battle of the Somme and rendered unable to ride a horse. Unwilling to be invalided out of the fighting, Park successfully hid his own medical records and joined the Royal Flying Corps as soon as his wounds were healed. He joined 48 Squadron in the summer of 1917 and rose to become its commander. During that time he was credited with some twenty kills and was shot down twice himself.

After the War, Park's career saw him rising from a flight lieutenant in the RAF through command posts on a number of RAF stations until in 1938 he became Senior Air Staff Officer at Fighter Command under Air Chief Marshal Sir Hugh Dowding. In April 1940, he was promoted to Air Vice Marshal and given command of 11 Group which was responsible for the air defences of London and South Eastern England. Within a month, he was organising the fighter sweeps over the beaches of Dunkirk as the B.E.F were evacuated. In the months to come, it would be Park's 11 Group that would be called upon to do the bulk of the fighting.

Air Vice Marshal Trafford Leigh-Mallory

Initially intending to be a lawyer, Trafford Leigh-Mallory volunteered for the Territorials when war broke out in 1914 and was wounded at the Second Battle of Ypres in 1915. He then signed up with the Royal Flying Corps where he flew missions over the Somme in 1916 with 7 Squadron. He later joined 5 and then 8 Squadron as its commander. He was not universally popular.

At war's end, Leigh-Mallory decided to stay with the RAF rather than pursue his intended legal career. By 1936 he was an air commodore and given charge of 12 Group protecting Central England in December 1937. Promotion to Air Vice Marshal came less than a year later, as Leigh-Mallory was above all an aggressively ambitious man with a good mastery of the more slippery side of politics.

Air Vice Marshal Keith Park, climbing into the cockpit of an aircraft

Messerschmitt Bf 109

When the Messerschmitt Bf 109 first started rolling off the production lines in February 1937, it was regarded as the finest fighter aircraft in the world. The Bf 109 was responsible for shooting down the bulk of Spitfires and Hurricanes lost during the Battle of Britain. It was both smaller and lighter than the Spitfire and Hurricane and faster and more manoeuvrable than the Hurricane. It could out dive the Spitfire and also out climb it at altitudes up to 20,000 feet, but the Spitfire and Hurricane possessed a better rate of turn - partly because Bf 109 pilots feared that their fighter's relatively weak wings would be ripped away if subjected to too much stress.

Messerschmitt Bf 110

Goering insisted that the Bf 110 be known as 'The Destroyer'. Before war broke out, he crowed that the Bf 110 was the finest fighter aircraft in the world. In 1936, when it first flew, that might have been true. By 1940, it was a very different story. It was still faster than a Hurricane and only a fraction slower than a Spitfire. Its front firing weapons – a combination of cannon and machine guns – unleashed a lethal spray of fire greater than anything other fighters could match. It carried three times more fuel than the Bf 109 – but it was still a failure. RAF pilots quickly realised that the rear gunner was often ineffective because he would either become disorientated or black out during the twists and turns of a dogfight. The aircraft suffered from poor acceleration qualities too and manoeuvred poorly. It soon became apparent to its elite crews that they were in a good deal of danger flying the aircraft. Among themselves they developed the tactic of flying in a defensive circle during dogfights with each aircraft just protecting the next. This rendered them useless as bomber escorts and indeed they often had to be provided with fighter escorts of their own.

Heinkel He 111

The veteran medium bomber of the Spanish Civil War was old by the time of the Battle of Britain. It had started off life as a Schnellbomber ('Fast Bomber') in the mid-1930s but its top speed was now easily matched and exceeded by both the Spitfire and the Hurricane. It consequently suffered a high percentage of losses during the Battle of Britain. Never particularly manoeuvrable to start with, the He 111's ability to take defensive action was further limited by its need to fly in tight formation for protection.

Junkers Ju 88

The Junkers Ju 88 was conceived in the mid-1930s as a Schnellbomber. The idea was that it would be able to outrun opposing fighter aircraft. Additionally, it would enjoy some abilities as a dive bomber.

It was, arguably, the best German bomber to see service in the Battle of Britain. It was faster, more manoeuvrable and had a greater range than both the Do 17 and He 111, despite having a heavier bomb payload. It could withstand considerable battle damage and dive out of trouble at a rate even a Spitfire couldn't match. Perhaps for those reasons, fewer Ju 88s were shot down during the Battle than any other German bomber type. One vulnerability was that it initially lacked enough defensive armaments as it was designed to outrun rather than outfight fighters. Experience of dogfights with the RAF quickly saw its onboard guns increased to six.

Dornier Do 17

They called the Do 17 the Fliegender Bleistift – the 'Flying Pencil'. Small and agile, particularly at low level, this light/medium bomber was intended to be a schnellbomber and outrun rather than outfight any fighter opposition. It fought in the Spanish Civil War in 1937 but was already being phased out by the time of the Battle of Britain and production of the Do 17 ended altogether during the Battle. A central weakness was its relatively small bomb-load. It also proved more effective as a bomber flying at low rather than higher levels.

JUNKERS JU 87 'STUKA'

The Stuka dive bomber with its distinctive gull-wing design and screaming 'Jericho Trumpet' siren was one of the mainstays of the Blitzkrieg in 1940, providing ferocious close air support for the panzers and troops on the ground. While it proved effective particularly against shipping in the opening weeks of the Battle of Britain, it soon began to show its vulnerability to RAF fighters. It was slow, unmanoeuvrable and lacking in defensive armaments. The rear gunner would often black out during particularly violent combat manoeuvres, giving any pursuing fighter an unopposed shot. Having suffered significant losses, the Stuka was largely withdrawn from the Battle of Britain by August 1940.

Hawker Hurricane

German pilots thought that 'Hurricane' was a very funny name for an aircraft. To their ears, in their language, it sounded like *'Whore Barges'.*

The Hurricane however would have the last laugh.

The true mainstay of the RAF fighter force during the summer of 1940, the Hurricane had been dreamed up by designer Sydney Camm in the early 1930s as a way of moving on from the traditional biplane fighter design. The first Hurricanes joined Fighter Command in 1937 and a total of 1,715 would serve during the Battle of Britain. Coming from a different era, the Hurricane was both slower than the Spitfire and unable to match its rate of climb, but could sustain quite major battle damage and still make it home. It is believed that Hurricanes were responsible for 4/5ths of all enemy aircraft shot down during the Battle of Britain.

I loved the Hurricane but I realised there was an awful lot to learn as we had come off biplanes. We had been flying Gladiators before then, which were the front line aircraft, and then to go along to the Hurricane was a challenge. We got more and more used to them and after a while we got to love them. There was something very basically strong about a Hurricane and you felt it was like a favourite car or something but there was tremendous strength in the aircraft and it was a perfect gun platform. It was just everything one ever wished for in an aeroplane.

DENNIS DAVID

Oh dear, I didn't like being shut in for a start with a closed hood over the top. But you got used to it pretty quickly. It meant it was a bit warmer. It was still bloody cold at altitude and of course the performance, the speed, was so much different from the old biplane that it was a great machine to fly. You each had your own aircraft and if your aircraft was being serviced you didn't fly so you had a bond between yourself and that particular aeroplane. If you had to fly somebody else's for some reason you didn't like it much.

PETE BROTHERS

I had flown super Furies, lovely aeroplanes, and Hawkers, lots of biplanes, but the Hurricane was new, it was a completely new aircraft. A new concept of flying too, we had to learn it, we had to learn this tremendous power which we had in front of us, but the take off in a Hurricane, in those days we had fixed two blade props, no variable pitch propellors, it was a very long take off and that used to worry me a bit, especially in those days we had flame trap troubles, which is not generally known today and meant the engine used to cut out about once every four or five take offs, cut out for a few seconds and then pick up again, you hoped, but your plan was to go straight on, as we were taught, if your engine cuts you keep straight on, you don't try to go sideways even if it meant going in to trees because you do less damage to yourself if you go straight at a tree. If you try to go sideways then you are asking for trouble or if you try to hold off you will stall.

DENNIS DAVID

A good stable aircraft. An easier aircraft to fly than the Spitfire, which I flew later, because you had a better view forward. Sitting in the Hurricane you were higher up and you got a good view forward for taking off or landing. It could take a lot of punishment and it could take a lot of machine gun bullets through the fuselage and the wings. A cannon shell through the wing of a Spitfire and it would fall to pieces. A Hurricane could be riddled with it and would still fly.

Tony Pickering

We flew Harts and Audax and things and then we went to Kidlington for a five hour refresher course on Harvards to give us some idea about undercarriages and flaps and boost controls, which of course the Hart didn't have. So five hours on Harvards and then I was posted to Sutton Bridge on the east coast of Norfolk to a Hurricane OTU and my first flight in a Hurricane was really straight forward. My instructor was a chap called Smallwood, Flying Officer Smallwood who would later become Air Chief Marshal Sir, but then he was a Flying Officer who had been in France and had been brought back as an instructor and he got me in the aeroplane and leaned over the side and more or less said you push that and you pull this and off you go. So off I went. I took off, flew around, came in and thought well this is great. Here I am, a Hurricane pilot.

Bob Foster

We flew Harvards at Brize Norton, at 2FTS, and they had a front gun and we did quite a lot of air to ground firing so that gave us an impression of how to aim and all that. The Harvard was a very good trainer and we went straight from the Harvard onto Hurricanes and the Hurricane was a very easy aeroplane to fly. It had wide undercarriage, ten feet, and the guns were very easily reloaded. In fact years later, when I got to know the designer of the Hurricane Sydney Camm, I was then at the Central Fighter Establishment and we were flying the Hunter, checking that out, and I used to go and see Sydney Camm and he was very bitter. He said the original design said you had to have an aeroplane with a ten foot wide undercarriage, over 90 gallons of fuel and the guns together so they could do a very rapid reload. You just took the cover off, put a new bunch of ammunition in and shut it up so the guns were reloaded inside two and a half minutes. He was very bitter. He used to say the Spitfire took eight minutes, had a narrower undercarriage and not enough fuel and they chose to prefer the Spitfire. He also told me the figures. If you consider the Messerschmitt 109, if that took 90 hours to build and the Hurricane took about 100 the Spitfire took 160 so in every way it was inferior but it was slightly faster but it could not outturn the 109 which the Hurricane did. The other extremely good thing about the Hurricane was if you were shot down and were doing a forced landing you landed wheels up and the large radiator underneath took most of the bounce out of the aeroplane and you could then just slide the hood back, knock the panel out and climb out and very little damage was done. In fact I'm told that very often they had aircraft which had force landed, a new airscrew was fitted on and various bits and you were flying again within 48 hours. The Hurricane in every way was a delightful aeroplane, very robust and good visibility.

John Ellacombe

We took off on the next morning, the Saturday morning, and went down to Hawkinge. I flew number two to Hector Proctor, the flight commander, who

a fortnight before had been a sergeant pilot with 501 Squadron, an ex boy, an ex-Halton boy, a flight lieutenant by that time, he'd gone up from sergeant pilot to acting flight lieutenant and he said to me 'Don't put your gun button on fire, sit behind me and watch what I do but you're not to use your gun button. I don't want to be shot out of the sky.' I think he thought I'd sit behind him and get too excited and press the button.'

TONY PICKERING

They were funny aircraft. You got used to them, you got to love them. They were very strong and you felt in the attack it would take anything you could do to it whereas the Spitfire I always had my doubts on because it was such a beautiful aeroplane, it just felt a little bit more, for instance if you did dive bombing, or sometimes in a dogfight, you do awful things to avoid getting bullets into you, you find yourself doing things the aircraft wasn't designed to take, but it did take it, the Hurricane took it and the Hurricane could out turn any aircraft. You'd get the speed down and you could pull it round in a tighter circle. This is what gave us the strong hand against the Me109. Of course, the Hurricane was the perfect bomber destroyer, it was the perfect aircraft for that, eight guns and you could do a lot with them

DENNIS DAVID

The Hurricane was very like a Hawker Hart, built in exactly the same way and it had what they called a thick high lift wing and there were no blanking plates between the wings where they joined the fuselage, it was all one particular piece of structure. Now there were three petrol tanks, the Hurricane had 97 gallons of fuel and the gravity tank which was in front of the pilot shielded by the engine and also by armour plate, and also by the pilot as well behind it. The two wing tanks held 30 gallons each, approximately, left and right of the pilot's feet. Now whenever you were attacked by German fighters as you were busy engaged shooting down the bombers the first thing that was hit was the two petrol tanks in your wings. They were not self sealing in those early days, they were just aluminium tanks, the fuel spilled out, caught fire which immediately came up behind the dashboard straight into the pilot's face so pilots flying Hurricanes were particularly prone to this eventuality. They were burned horribly about the hands and face and there are so many examples of that. In fact most of the people who were shot down and burned were flying Hurricanes mainly because of the manner in which the Hurricane was constructed. When the Hurricane II came out they had self sealing tanks which made a little bit of difference but still you were horribly vulnerable as we found in Malta because the 109s continued to shoot us down.

TOM NEIL

OPP. PAGE LEFT: K5083, the prototype Hurricane with Hawker Chief Test Pilot, George Bulman, at the controls. **OPP. PAGE CENTRE:** A view from above clearly showing the shape of the Hurricane. **CENTRE LEFT AND RIGHT:** Women at work on the wing and fuselage skins at the Hawker factory in KIngston. **ABOVE CENTRE:** Working on the propeller of a later production Hurricane. **ABOVE RIGHT:** The Hurricane production line in the Gloster factory at Hucclecote

Supermarine Spitfire

Its ancestor was a champion seaplane racer and R. J. Mitchell's revolutionary design was still regarded as incredibly glamorous when the Spitfire took to the skies during the Battle of Britain. The mystique remains today. The prototype first flew in March 1936 and it first saw service with RAF Fighter Command in 1938. Behind the scenes, manufacturing plants raced to get the new fighter off the production line and, by July 1940 19 full RAF Squadrons had been equipped with Spitfires. The first Spitfire kill occurred on 16 October 1939 – barely a month since war had broken out – when a Spitfire Mk1 shot down a Heinkel He 111 bomber over the Firth of Forth in Scotland.

The thing flew me to start with. I can see it. I can remember walking out to it and looking at it and there was this lithe single-seater, almost delicate in appearance, no instructor in the back of that thing. You had to get in and fly it all with a maximum of 140 hours flying and I can remember my oxygen mask as I walked banging, I can feel it banging across my face and the two ground crew looking at me as if to say 'Oh God, another sprog'. I can also remember, almost with resignation, taxying out down wind and turning into wind and thinking 'well there's no excuse now. I might as well get going' and I opened the throttle and the acceleration was something I'd never experienced. The next thing I knew the thing had leaped into the air with me hanging on to it. But once I got it into the air, and the aircraft cleaned up, I got it up to about 10,000, it was a lovely day with lots of fluffy white clouds around, and I remember floating round the sky in this wonderful aeroplane and the thought came into my brain that I wanted to do something and somehow the thought transmitted itself to the aeroplane and it did it and then of course there was the question of getting over the euphoria and getting it back on the ground. It was the most important part of the sortie and I undershot a bit because, in Harvards, where I was trained, you came in with a lot of motor but if you did that in a Spitfire, with wheels and flaps down, it assumed a tail down attitude, quite stable, didn't drop a wing on you or anything like that, and that meant ten feet of nose came up and you couldn't see ahead. I remember seeing, I can see it now, the hedge going by underneath and there was the grass coming up quickly and I can remember pulling the stick back and she went straight on the ground. Not a bump anywhere, stable, a lovely, lovely pilot's aeroplane. The aeroplane flew me on take off and landing but I had quite a lot of fun with it when I was in the air so it's very, very vivid.

Geoffrey Wellum

I felt about the Spitfire that it was a beautiful aeroplane, it flew very nicely, it was quite fast and there was a good chance that you could shoot down some enemy aircraft. There was also quite a good chance, if you learned to fly it properly, you could avoid being shot down. I think every time I got into a Spitfire I felt a sense of joy because it was a lovely aircraft to fly

---

Terence Kane

One morning the ATA arrived to fly our Blenheims away and they arrived flying in Spitfires. We were given the order to learn to fly these so we were all ready to get into our Spitfires the very next day. We were told to go and draw our pilot's notes, swat up and when we were done to report back to

Ground crew wait by their 19 Squadron Spitfires

the flight commander down at dispersal and you would be taken by him, take a seat in a Spitfire, get strapped in, have your parachute strapped on and your Sutton harness strapped on, you'd be given a tour of the cockpit, told what to expect and what not to expect on your first solo and the fact that you were going to swing on take off in a certain way and if you didn't correct the swing you'd finish up in the hedge. Having taken all this on board, and being pilots with, I suppose, 160 hours experience behind us we found going solo no trouble at all. It was just a thrill that everybody who's ever flown a Spitfire expected it to be. After flying Blenheims you'd find speeds like 300 on the clock. Here was an aircraft that at the slightest touch would do what you asked it to do. We liked flying our Blenheims but then to be given the opportunity of flying Spitfires it was something else entirely, something beyond what we could have hoped for

KEITH LAWRENCE

I wanted to fly fighters, not necessarily Spitfires but we went on to Spitfires at Hawarden in Cheshire and just had a fortnight to switch to Spitfires which was very interesting because after the Master opening up the throttle of the Spitfire was like a kick in the back. You could really feel the boost and they were nice and light and easy to fly except they had this pump action for getting the wheels up, bringing the flaps up. You could always tell the newcomers by watching the aircraft going round the circuit leapfrogging as people tried to pump the flaps up or down ready for their landing.

DOUG NICHOLLS

The Spitfire meant a tremendous amount. The Spitfire was a wonderful aeroplane that took you into battle and, God willing, it brought you back again. You didn't like to fly anybody else's Spitfire. You wanted to fly yours and the ground crews didn't like another pilot flying their aeroplane. It was part of the team, the fitter, the rigger, you and the aeroplane. I used to talk to it. When I was in combat, for some reason, I used to shout, yell, all sorts of obscenities, God knows what it did. Black crosses? What are you doing over here? I used to yell at the top of my voice, normally when I was frightened which was continually.

GEOFFREY WELLUM

Bloody marvellous – you felt you'd been flying it all your life – so training must have been some good. The feel of sheer joy that here was an aircraft which did everything you wanted, if you wanted to get up there fast you went up there fast. She was so precise….so precise and lovely.

DAVID DENCHFIELD

It had no nasty habits whatsoever. I got into a spin in cloud one day trying to be clever and I came out and there was the earth, I thought it shouldn't be there, straight down, and I took corrective action and a single seater fighter, high powered, it just came out like that. I did a lot of stupid things in a Spitfire because I was stupid, precocious I suppose, and it got me out every time, totally stable, beautiful, beautiful aeroplane.

GEOFFREY WELLUM

Well it was simply because of this, one it was powerful, two it was very manoeuvrable, three it answered the controls readily and easily and therefore it enabled you to get out of trouble mainly. I wasn't a great fighter pilot but I was a great survivor and I found that I could usually escape from trouble.

JIMMY CORBIN

It was lovely to fly but it had two disadvantages. One was that if you tried to pull up after you'd landed because you were short of runway or grass many people tipped up on the nose because the centre of gravity was so near the wheels. The other thing was that you couldn't see straight ahead on the ground at all and people collided with other people. In the air the disadvantage was that if you had to take a deflection shot of anything like 15 degrees or more, if you were taking a correct shot, you wouldn't be seeing your target at all because it would be underneath the nose. It could have been a so much better aeroplane if you'd been able to see over the nose. In every other respect it was wonderful.

ALLAN WRIGHT

The smell of the oil and the 100 octane. A Spitfire had its own smell, It was all part of it. Of course you didn't realise and you got used to it but it had its own smell, its own character. Each had its own idiosyncracies but you got to know it and had it trimmed as you wanted it. You knew how to get the best out of the engine which never faltered. Thank God for Rolls Royce.

GEOFFREY WELLUM

LEFT: The Rolls Royce Merlin II engine as used in the early Mk 1 Hurricanes and Spitfires. **SECOND LEFT:** The legendary pair that created a legendary aircraft, RJ Mitchell, of Vickers-Supermarine and Sir Henry Royce. **CENTRE LEFT:** A Merlin engine installed in a Spitfire. **CENTRE RIGHT:** Senior RAF officers being shown the Spitfire prototype, K5054. **SECOND RIGHT:** K9787, the first production Spitfire which first flew on 14 May 1938

BOULTON PAUL DEFIANT

On 19 July, the RAF suffered dreadful losses when they tried to introduce their Boulton Paul Defiant fighters into combat over the Channel. 12 Defiants of 141 Squadron were ordered to intercept a formation of Ju 87s attacking shipping off Folkestone. Three of the 12 failed to make it to the intercept due to mechanical problems. They were the lucky ones. The remaining nine Defiants were pounced on by 16 Bf 109s of JG51 and torn to shreds. With no forward guns, they proved totally vulnerable to the Messerschmitts. Six were shot down in just a matter of minutes. Only three managed to escape as Hurricanes from 111 Squadron swooped in to rescue them. The three Defiants limped home, one missing its gunner who had bailed out over the Channel and subsequently drowned in the water.

LEFT: Fred Barker and his pilot Ted Thorne **SECOND LEFT** of 264 Squadron, formed the most successful Defiant crew shooting down 12 enemy aircraft during Dunkirk and the Battle of Britain. **MIDDLE LEFT:** K8310, the Defiant original prototype, first flew on 11 August 1937 **MIDDLE RIGHT:** Line up of production Defiants ready for delivery on 17 January 1940 **RIGHT AND SECOND RIGHT:** Boulton Paul test pilot, Robert Lindsay Neale pictured before a Defiant test flight.

They had no forward guns so you only had the turret rotating on the top. It would be alright I suppose if you could sneak up on a German bomber and get a side shot at him but they weren't really fast enough for that. You couldn't get any height quickly in them so I'm afraid they were not a great success.

DOUG NICHOLLS

After we'd been made operational on the Blenheims, we were told we were going to get the Defiant. It was a single engined aeroplane. It was a brand new aircraft for us and we just thought that this was marvellous, a step forward. When they first started arriving in we had to be converted from the twin engined, which I'd always been trained on, to the single engined aircraft. To do that we had a couple of Harvards so we flew the Harvard to get back to single engines and then an old Fairey Battle came along and with that we did circuits and bumps and my recollection is that you took the thing off, you were told not to bother to bring your wheels up, as you had to wind them up as I recall in the early ones, just to fly around and land it. In other words to make sure you could take a single engined aeroplane off, make a circuit and come in and land. After that we got straight into the Defiants and there you were, piloting a brand new aeroplane and my thoughts were, this is magnificent and giving no real thought to the fact that we didn't have guns to fire forward and that we had the chap on the back in the turret.

JOHN GARD'NER

It was very formidable to fight with, a very formidable aeroplane. Now when it arrived, all beautiful, shiny, new with a huge gun turret with those massive-looking guns sticking out. It was exciting but I recall that some people found it a bit difficult. We lost a couple of chaps who stalled in off the end of the runway simply during the time we were converting.

JOHN GARD'NER

Plan of Action
The Luftwaffe

Luftflottes II and III, now stationed on captured airfields in occupied France and Belgium, would lead the assault across the Channel and over Southern England, with Luftflotte V in Denmark and Norway providing further striking power across the North Sea.

Goering's initial plan was to provoke RAF Fighter Command to come up and fight in large numbers – and to be destroyed quickly and decisively in a short series of massive air engagements. With RAF Fighter Command destroyed, Britain would be defenceless and would either have to sue for peace or face invasion. The Luftwaffe had the advantage of numbers and, in the Bf 109, a world class fighter more than capable of taking on the Spitfire and Hurricane.

Plan of Action
The Royal Air Force

Dowding had correctly guessed the Luftwaffe's plan of attack and had worked out a way to best face it. He decided to use what was known as the Fabian System – only putting small numbers of aircraft into the air at any given time to meet the enemy, a tactic which avoided large scale actions but which would gradually wear down the Luftwaffe while conserving men and machines. Dowding understood that, if he could successfully hold out for just a few months, Britain would be saved by winter. No seaborne invasion could be launched so late in the year and Britain would have perhaps an extra six months to better prepare for the Germans when they came.

Luftwaffe Strength (July 1940)

Luftflotte I & II

Bombers 2,000

Fighters 980

Reconnaissance 140

Luftflotte V

Bombers 130

Fighters 30

Reconnaissance 30

RAF Strength (July 1940)

10, 11, 12 and 13 Groups Fighter Command

650 fighter aircraft

1,300 pilots

Temporary Filter Room set up at Fighter Command HQ at Bentley Priory, Stanmore, Middlesex

WICK
INVERNESS
KYLE
ELGIN
ABERDEEN
FORT WILLIAM
OBAN
PERTH
DUNDEE
STIRLING
GLASGOW
EDINBURGH
LANARK
GALASHIELS
BERWICK
AYR
DUMFRIES
CARLISLE
NEWCASTLE
BELFAST
WHITEHAVEN
PENRITH
MIDDLESBROUGH
BARROW
HARROGATE
YORK
HULL
BRADFORD
LEEDS
PRESTON
MANCHESTER
LIVERPOOL
GRIMSBY
DONCASTER
SHEFFIELD
LINCOLN
COLWYN BAY
CHESTER
BANGOR
STOKE ON TRENT
DERBY
NOTTINGHAM
BOSTON
KINGS-LYNN
NORWICH
DUBLIN
LEICESTER
PETERBOROUGH
BIRMINGHAM
COVENTRY
RUGBY
NORTHAMPTON
BEDFORD
CAMBRIDGE
BURY St EDS
IPSWICH
COLCHESTER
EVESHAM
BANBURY
AYLESBURY
CHELTENHAM
GLOUCESTER
OXFORD
CHELMSFORD
SWINDON
NEWBURY
READING
LONDON NORTH
LONDON CENTRAL
LONDON SOUTH
MAIDSTONE
CANTERBURY
BASINGSTOKE
GUILDFORD
HORSHAM
TUNBRIDGE WELLS
SALISBURY
PORTSMOUTH
BOURNEMOUTH
BRIGHTON

July 1940 – Kanalkampf

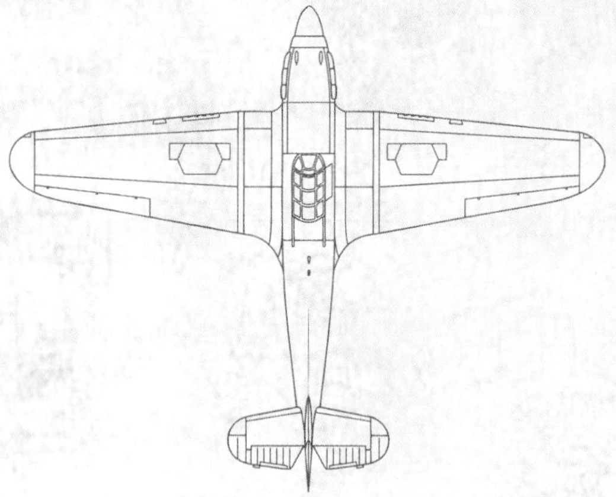

The Battle of Britain officially began on Wednesday 10 July 1940 – but that's a fairly arbitrary date. At the time, it was regarded as a day like any other and for many years, the start date of the battle was given as 8 August in official records and text books. Indeed, on 8 August, the RAF 'Order of the Day' told pilots *'The Battle of Britain is about to begin, Members of the Royal Air Force, the fate of generations lies in your hands.'*

By 1 July, the Luftwaffe were already engaged in serious missions over Britain. On that day, bombers from Luftflotte V hit Hull as well as Wick in Scotland. Cardiff was bombed two days later and the following day Stuka dive bombers went after a convoy stretched out between Cherbourg and Bournemouth, sinking five merchant ships. Portland Harbour was attacked later the same day. Throughout this time, the Luftwaffe was also actively engaged in minelaying operations around the coast. On 8 July, Spitfires from 54 Squadron had tangled with a mixed formation of Bf 110s and Bf 109s and had lost two aircraft in the ensuing dogfight. On the 9th, Hurricanes of 43 Squadron fought an inconclusive duel with Bf 110s.

What made 10 July different was the weather. During the first week or so of July, the weather over the Channel had been fairly inclement. On the 10th, just before noon, the cloud finally started to lift – and the Luftwaffe soon came out in force embarking on the first day of what they called Kanalkampf (*'Channel Struggle'*). Radar detected a large body of enemy aircraft heading for a convoy codenamed Bread in the straits between Dover and Dungeness. RAF fighters were ordered to scramble in response – the Spitfires of 74 Squadron out of Hornchurch, Hurricanes of 56 Squadron from North Weald, 111 Squadron from Croydon, 32 Squadron from Biggin Hill, who were already out on patrol and – later on – six Spitfires from 64 Squadron out of Kenley. Facing them across the Channel were 24 Do 17s

19 Squadron pilots scramble at Duxford aerodrome

DEFENDING THE CONVOYS

32 Squadron, experienced after the Battle of France and Dunkirk, were in the forefront of the operations to protect convoys in the English Channel, Pete Brothers recalls.

We were the front line. Obviously anything coming in from the Continent was going to enter Kent first and, of course, we were close to the channel where there was an awful lot of our shipping which the Germans took exception to and started to bomb so we had to fly convoy patrols, patrolling over the convoy, which became exciting when the Germans decided to do the same and bomb it so we had quite a lot of engagements in that respect before they ever started flying over the UK or entering our airspace. Of course, Hawkinge was ideal as you'd get to Hawkinge, top up with fuel so that you were absolutely full and ready to go and go off on patrol or on the odd occasion we got scrambled because a convoy was being attacked and the previous squadron guarding it had obviously had to return and so there was a gap in the cover. That was quite exciting because the Germans were using Stuka dive bombers which were cat's meat if you could get at them but there was usually a heavy patrol of 109 fighters to protect the Stukas so every time you picked on a Stuka, before you got a chance to shoot at it you got a 109 behind you so you had to take great care. One of the things one found irritating, to quite a degree, was to fly back from a convoy patrol having been jolly busy engaging German aircraft, and sweep over the beaches which were littered with girls in their swimming costumes sunning themselves. It made you want to shout loudly 'Hey, there's a war on. Get stuck in.' That was quite interesting. The difference, if you like, between us at the time who were busy fighting and people on the ground who were sunbathing and enjoying themselves.

Doug Nicholls, flying with 151 Squadron out of RAF Digby in Lincolnshire, was at readiness to patrol the convoys when they reached the North Sea.

151 at Digby was on line for the Midlands and the bomber streams used to come over this way. Later on the Germans had this beam which came over Lincolnshire towards Birmingham and Sheffield and so on and we also were involved in convoy protection which was another bone of contention because all the times we'd been out and patrolled a convoy and then we've seen something suspicious coming up on the side. At first it was just a question of signals by Verey light and then later on we got radio contact and we could ask for permission to cross the convoy and usually permission was given so we would cross it at right angles because some of those convoys were probably 20 miles long and it would take a hell of a lot of time to go round, by which time the enemy bomber could have done his damage and gone so we used to go over the middle of the convoy, 'Oh yes, permission granted' and we'd get over the convoy and all hell would be let loose. Its no good getting permission from the navy, they're just bloody fire happy. I met a fellow in a local pub shortly afterwards who had been on these convoys. I said 'I'm glad to have met you, who's bloody side are you on' which caused a little bit of a stir in the pub.

escorted by 30 Bf 110s and 20 or more Bf 109s.

111 Squadron hit the Dornier formation hard over Folkestone while the others went after their fighter escorts. The resulting massed air battle was a definite victory for the RAF. Two Dornier bombers were destroyed and no less than ten of their fighter escorts shot down. Only one ship in the convoy was sunk. However, the day did see the RAF's first official combat casualty of the Battle of Britain. PO Thomas 'Peter' Higgs of 111 Squadron, a 23-year-old Hurricane pilot from Oldham, was blazing away on the tail of a Do 17 when he was bounced by a Bf 109. Surprised, he accidentally collided with the bomber and his fighter spun away out of control and minus a wing. Higgs managed to bail out but died in the water. His body was washed up in Holland a month later. The stricken Dornier also went down into the Channel where two of its crew were rescued. The 'first day' also saw formations of Ju 88s fly almost completely unopposed to bomb Swansea and Falmouth.

On Thursday 11 July, the weather deteriorated again, limiting the combat sorties the Luftwaffe could launch. The most serious clash

occurred off Portland, where six Spitfires from 609 Squadron at Middle Wallop were guided by radar onto a formation of Ju 87s hunting a Channel convoy. As they prepared to pounce on the Stukas, they were in turn bounced by a superior force of Bf 109s and two Spitfires were shot down. A Hurricane of 501 Squadron was also lost. All three pilots were killed. Hurricanes of 601 Squadron from Tangmere joined the fight over Portland later and accounted for two Ju 87s and two Bf 110s. British convoys were attacked throughout the day, especially in the Solent, by flights of Ju 87s and He 111s.

The clashes of 10 and 11 July set the pattern for pretty much the rest of July. German bombers – in small or large numbers – would go after shipping in the Channel with or without fighter escorts. In turn, radar would guide relatively small RAF fighter formations against them with varying degrees of success. To the Luftwaffe, everything was going to plan. They were making an impact on British shipping while successfully enticing the RAF fighters up to be attacked by their fighter escorts.

On 19 July, the RAF suffered dreadful losses when they tried to introduce their Boulton Paul Defiant fighters into combat over the Channel. 12 Defiants of 141 Squadron were ordered to intercept a formation of Ju 87s attacking shipping off Folkestone. Three of the twelve failed to make it to the intercept due to mechanical problems. They were the lucky ones. The remaining nine Defiants were pounced on by sixteen Bf 109s of JG51 and torn to shreds. With no forward guns, they proved totally vulnerable to the Messerschmitts. Six were shot down in just a matter of minutes. Only three managed to escape as Hurricanes from 111 Squadron swooped in to rescue them. The three Defiants limped home, one missing its gunner who had bailed out over the Channel and subsequently drowned in the water.

The first nine days of combat confused the Germans. They could not understand why the RAF was limiting its fighter response. The optimists among them believed that the RAF must be much weaker than anticipated. The pessimists decided to wait and see. Some British commanders were baffled too, especially those in the navy. As far as they could see, the RAF were simply not doing enough to protect shipping.

Spitfire Mk1s of 611 Squadron at Digby in Lincolnshire

Dowding had asked the government during the month to re-route all convoys away from the Channel so that his fighters would not have to fly missions protecting them. It seemed a waste of vital men and machines if there was an alternative. Churchill had personally refused his request, saying that it would amount to a loss of faith if British ships could not use British waters. However, by 23 July, the threat to British convoys had become so serious that many were indeed routed away from the Channel and instead sent northward along the east coast and around Scotland before heading out into the Atlantic. This also meant that any bombers trying to intercept them would have to do so without fighter escorts as the distances were too great and would find themselves more vulnerable to British fighter defences.

Convoys were still the Luftwaffe's target of choice whenever possible though and on Wednesday 24 July, Dorniers went after one negotiating the Thames Estuary. 54 Squadron Spitfires temporarily operating out of Rochford and 64 Squadron Spitfires were scrambled to meet them just before 8am. Three 54 Squadron Spitfires were shot down by the gunners on board the German bombers for no German losses. At 11 am, another formation of Dorniers moved in on the same convoy and 54 Squadron went looking for them, desperate for a rematch. They found themselves facing 18 Dorniers escorted by over 40 Bf 109 fighters – and quickly called for help. Spitfires from 65 Squadron at Hornchurch and 610 Squadron from Gravesend scrambled in response and intercepted the enemy almost directly over Margate. Townsfolk were stunned to see massed dogfighting over their heads. Dorniers, panicked by the Spitfires, dived desperately to almost sea level to escape their guns and were reported to be almost clipping the roofs of Margate's grand seafront hotels as they fled. A German fighter pilot fell to his death into the town as his parachute failed to open and a doomed Spitfire narrowly avoided slamming straight into the Royal Esplanade on the seafront. At the last minute the pilot – 24-year-old fighter ace Johnny Allen DFC - managed to pull up and avoid the crowded area before exploding in a fireball in the air. In total, three Dorniers were shot down as well as four Bf 109s. The legendary Adolf Galland flew his first combat sortie during the battle that day and the ferocious flying of the Spitfire pilots proved to him that this would be no easy walkover for the Luftwaffe.

The Luftwaffe went after another convoy on Thursday 25 July. Naval escorts called desperately for RAF air cover in the early morning hours as their convoy was simultaneously hit by Ju 87 dive bombers and nimble but deadly E-boats of the Kriegsmarine as it entered the Dover Straits. Heavy German guns firing from occupied France added to the confusion. 32 and 615 Squadron Hurricanes tangled with Bf 109s at almost sea level, while 54 Squadron Spitfires found themselves badly outnumbered by more Messerschmitts. As the RAF fought to get through the fighter cover and at the dive bombers, the Stukas helped inflict heavy losses on the convoy. Eleven coal ships were sunk along with two Royal Navy destroyer escorts. By 2.30pm, 40 Ju 88s had joined in the assault, protected by more than 50 fresh Bf 109s. The RAF found themselves badly overstretched and the Spitfires and Hurricanes they could scramble were vastly outnumbered. In desperation, the RAF pilots flew directly at the bomber formations at full throttle to break them up and disrupt them. The tactic worked and the attack dispersed. However, German fighters and bombers returned later to complete their task. Of the 21 ships in the convoy, only two got through.

Attacks on convoys continued until the weekend, when authorities took stock and realised that naval and convoy operations in the Channel were becoming almost impossible. It was decided that Dover would have to be abandoned as an advanced base, all destroyers would be moved to safety and the RAF would have to be relied upon almost exclusively to provide protection to the convoys. As if to prove the point, three naval destroyers were lost on Saturday 27 July alone.

Even as British authorities struggled to maintain control of the Channel, the Germans were trying to come to terms with their combat losses, which were far far higher than had been anticipated. By the end of 23 July Luftwaffe losses were 85 aircraft to Fighter Command's 45. On Sunday 28 July alone, the Luftwaffe lost 18 warplanes. Furthermore, much to their surprise, British Blenheim bombers were making daring solo retaliatory raids on their French airfields, not achieving much in the way of damage but succeeding in keeping everyone on edge.

By the end of the month, it became clear to the German High Command that their tactics were not working. Goering had anticipated breaking the strength of the RAF in a relatively small number of decisive large-scale aerial battles over the Channel. He thought that the RAF would come out further on intercepts than they did. He thought they would fly in greater numbers than they did. Now, after the first month's combat, Goering found himself looking at 193 pilots and bomber crew confirmed dead and a further 302 listed as missing. 216 Luftwaffe aircraft had been shot down during July. These figures did not augur well compared to RAF losses of 77 aircraft destroyed and 67 pilots and crew killed. He would have to try something else.

The Dornier 215 was used sparingly during the Battle of Britain but was used for convoy attacks in July

Slaughter of the Innocents

John Gard'ner was the last survivor of that raid and remembered it well.

On 19 July we were ordered on patrol, there were 12 aircraft. In the event three of them, in the run ups, found there was something wrong with the engines and the answer was that only nine got airborne. We were organised into the vics of three, and I do know that the intercom was poor between the pilot and the air gunner and as far as hearing anything going on being ordered by your squadron leader everything was done, more or less, by hand signals. The radio communication was almost non-existent.

Now our tactics, if we were going to be attacked, were to go into a circle and I recall that, when going back to our training in Scotland, it was the only tactics we were asked to do. If you were going out on patrol you'd fly in these vic formations of three, your leader would tell you to go into line astern and from line astern we would go into a circle and I remember being tail Charlie, and the greatest difficulty was to keep in the circle as you were pulling harder and harder G to maintain it. I don't recall ever having the air gunner fire the guns so when it came to the actual battle, when I realised I was being hit, I described it as a thumping noise on the aircraft but thinking back it could well have been the air gunner firing off a burst before he was obviously hit.

The squadron took off from Hawkinge to patrol the Channel convoy.

Literally we were going happily and suddenly thump, thump thump and I saw tracers coming through. I have recollection of tracers coming under my armpits and going out through the front of the aircraft. There was what I thought I heard at the time, this thumping noise, then suddenly there was a smell of oil and cordite, this is why I think

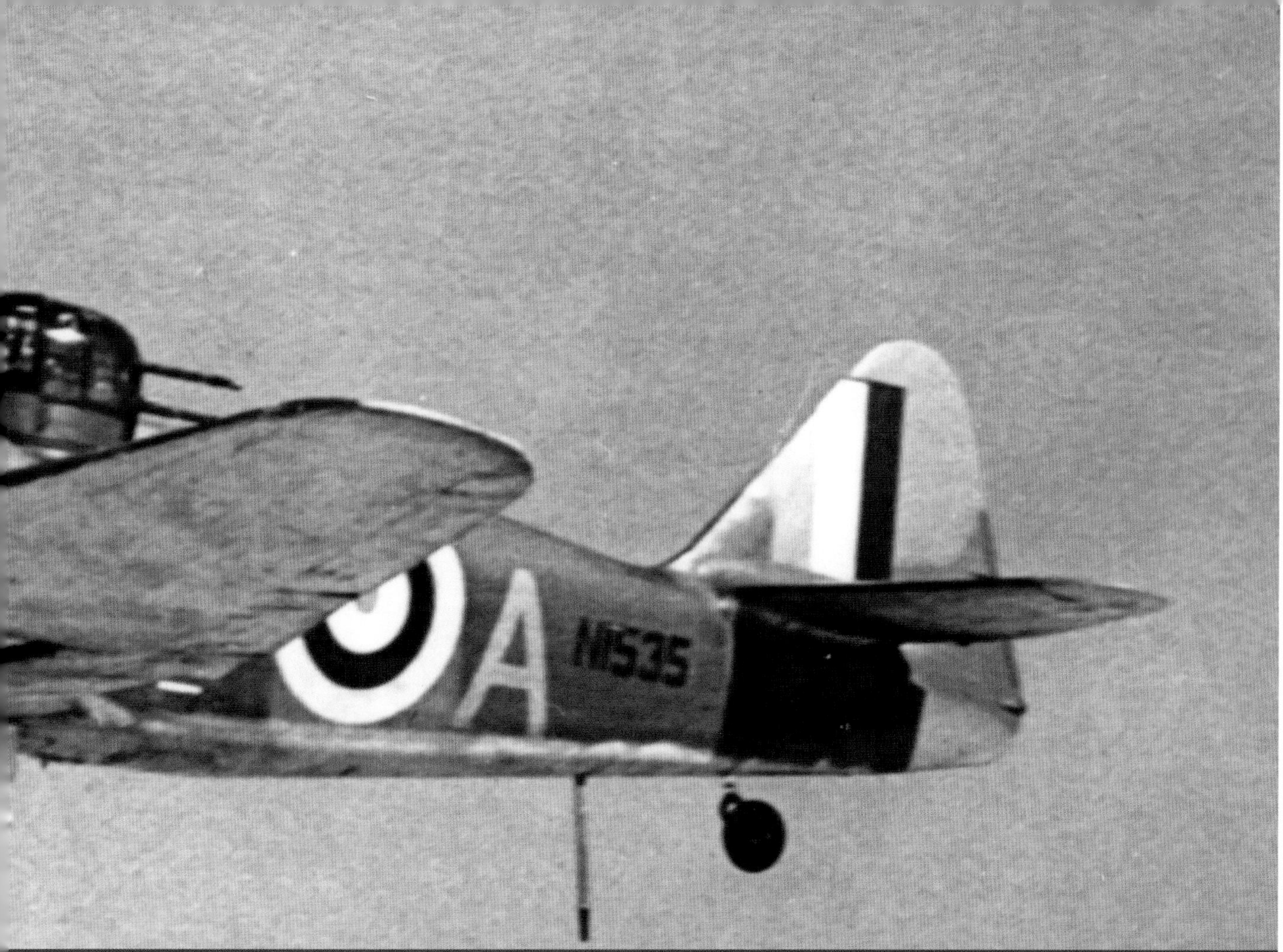

the gunner got a burst off, and that was it. Suddenly my engine just stopped, nothing there, and the other thing I felt was 'God, I'm being hit' and I turned over quickly and the rudder bar felt floppy at my feet. I turned over and went down as steep as I could go, I said 'How do you feel?' to the back, no response, so down I went and it just seemed to me there I was, suddenly nothing to be seen anywhere. We weren't very high, 8,000 to 10,000 feet if that and I'd made that in one big swoop. I saw a naval vessel so I thought I'll try and land beside it and I went by it at quite a speed, I overshot it, and I thought I'll try going round again. It's a miracle to me, I don't know how I kept the aeroplane level because I could still feel I wasn't getting anything out of the rudder. I know from the pictures that I came around in a descending swoop, streaming black smoke out of the back and that was how it was pictured and as I got close to the water I thought 'I'm going into the water and I've got to get out of here quickly' and for some stupid reason I undid my straps thinking I'd got to get out quickly. Well obviously I hit the water and the next thing I knew was I was in black water. I'd obviously been knocked out and the aeroplane had sunk but I was able to get myself out of the cockpit. I could see light above and I managed to get myself to the top and then I saw blood all round the place and I realised my face was hanging down and then I blacked out again. I was picked up by a motor torpedo boat and again I remember coming to and saying to the chaps for some reason or other my flying boots had come off and whether it was my imagination or whether they were actually there I can picture my two flying boots side by side in the water and in those days we wore those beautiful shiny black ones which were changed later on and I said 'Will you please get my flying boots out?' and nobody took any notice of that so I faded out. I came to next time and I was lying in hospital in Dover. I was swathed in bandages, feeling very sorry for myself.

During our battle I didn't see a thing. I had no idea who hit us. I saw no other aeroplanes, The sky was empty as far as I was concerned and talking about seeing the battle from then onwards I do remember lying in the hospital, I had a bed right beside the window and I saw lots of vapour trails and I said 'That's where the battle is and here am I here.' I felt a bit unhappy about that.

DIRECTIVE 16

As England, in spite of her hopeless military situation, still shows no signs of willingness to come to terms, I have decided to prepare, and if necessary to carry out, a landing operation against her. The aim of this operation is to eliminate the English Motherland as a base from which the war against Germany can be continued, and, if necessary, to occupy the country completely.'

Throughout June and July, the Nazis had been trying to sound Britain out about a peace settlement. They got nowhere. Hitler decided to develop further his invasion plans to show that he wasn't bluffing. On 16 July, he issued Directive 16 – instructions for the invasion of England. The document set out the plans for a *'surprise crossing on a wide front'* from Ramsgate in the east to an unspecified area west of the Isle of Wight, with the Luftwaffe acting in the role of artillery support. The invasion would be codenamed 'Seelowe' or Sea Lion and all preparations should be completed by the middle of August. Before such an invasion could be launched, however, five criteria would need to be met:

- **The English Air Force must be so reduced morally and physically that it is unable to deliver any significant attack against the German crossing.**
- **Mine-free channels must be cleared.**
- **The Straits of Dover must be closely sealed off with minefields on both flanks; also the Western entrance to the Channel approximately on the line Alderney-Portland.**
- **Strong forces of coastal artillery must command and protect the forward coastal area.**
- **It is desirable that the English navy be tied down shortly before the crossing, both in the North Sea and in the Mediterranean (by the Italians).**
- **For this purpose we must attempt even now to damage English home-based naval forces by air and torpedo attack as far as possible.**
- **Everything should be in place for August.**

It's fair to say that Hitler composing his instructions seemed somehow less than convinced or committed, using the phrase *'if necessary'* twice in the first paragraph. Even now, he hoped that the English establishment would crumble when faced with a viable invasion threat and sue for peace. A coalition of appeasers, fascist sympathisers, nationalists and peace activists would then run the country as a German vassal state while Hitler got on with attacking his true enemy – the Soviet Union.

Hitler made his final peace offer on 19 July. The next day, when asked what he would say to Hitler, Churchill replied, *'I do not propose to say anything in reply to Herr Hitler's speech – not being on speaking terms with him'.* The German press portrayed the British rejection of terms as 'a war crime'.

Adolf Hitler in conversation with Robert Ley, Ferdinand Porsche and Hermann Goering

Preparations for 'Sea Lion'

Spurred into action by the Fuhrer's directive, the Kriegsmarine and Wehrmacht started to make plans. It was first suggested that the initial wave of the German invasion force would comprise 260,000 men, 30,000 vehicles and 60,000 horses over 3 days. The Army proposed an invasion along a 237 mile front – and the Navy very quickly said that was impossible. Both services continued to fight amongst themselves through July and August 1940, with the army plans becoming less and less ambitious as the Navy criticised them. Rather than fighting on a 237 mile front, the Wehrmacht were forced to reduce their plans to attack along a 100 mile front instead. This was later reduced to 90 miles.

Everyone who looked at the task thought – in their hearts – that it was next to impossible. For a start, there were next to no boats to ferry men, machines and equines across the Channel. The solution planners came up with was to commandeer inland barges from the canals and waterways all across Northern Europe to act as impromptu troop transports. Many were ridiculously – and dangerously – ill-suited to a sea crossing and a high proportion had no power of their own. They would have to be towed across the Channel by tugs. In addition to the barges, coastal steamers were to be seized and tourist car ferries commandeered.

No one was particularly convinced about it all. Hitler could see some faults, the Kriegsmarine were desperately nervous of doing their part, the army chopped and changed its plans to accommodate opposing views and General Halder, architect of the Blitzkrieg, said in private that he might as well just feed his troops into a giant sausage machine.

Through the summer and into the autumn, a rag tag fleet began to assemble in ports all along the Channel coasts, with troop formations in tents close by, just waiting for the orders to go. Everything hinged on Goering and the Luftwaffe being able to destroy the RAF in good time.

August 1940 - Adlerangriff

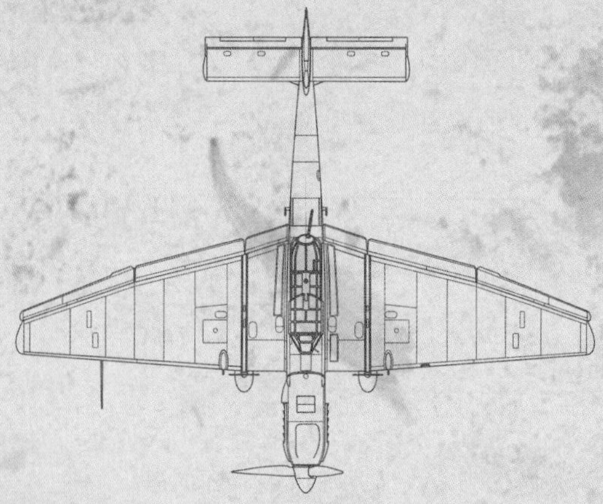

Just as Hitler was issuing Directive 17, Goering was addressing a meeting of Luftflotte commanders in the Hague. He explained to them that the present tactics weren't working, but RAF fighter numbers were reported to be small and a definitive air engagement should finish them off with ease. The following day, Goering began work on meeting Hitler's instructions and to change the focus of the offensive. As he did so, sporadic attacks were made against the convoys but overall the skies over Britain were largely quiet due to a combination of bad weather and changing Luftwaffe priorities.

On 5 August, a convoy was attacked off the straits of Dover by Ju 88s with a Bf 109 escort. As they attacked, they were challenged by the Hurricanes of 151 Squadron, who succeeded in shooting down one of the fighter escorts and damaging another of the bombers. The attack was the exception rather than the rule though and, by Wednesday 7 August, British authorities were so encouraged by the reduced Luftwaffe activity over the Channel that they decided to give the go ahead for a large coal convoy codenamed Peewit to run the gauntlet from the Thames Estuary through the Dover Straits (now nicknamed 'Hellfire Corner') to Swanage. Nine warships were assigned as escorts and barrage balloons attached to the ships for extra protection. German shipping radar at Wissant on the Cap Blanc Nez saw them coming.

The first attack, at night, was by German E-boats, slipping in amongst the merchant ships and firing torpedoes. The convoy broke up in confusion, with two ships colliding and sinking. The next morning, as the convoy pulled itself together and headed west once more, 145 Squadron flew escort and fought off occasional raids by Ju 87s. A massed attack against the convoy was launched at noon as it passed south of the Isle of Wight. It was hit first by 30 Bf 109s, firing incendiary bullets to burst the covering barrage balloons. Then in came almost 60 Ju 87 dive bombers, shielded by a 20-plane BF 110 escort. 145 Squadron out of Tangmere caught the Stukas mid-dive and managed to dispose

Luftwaffe air gunner on a bombing mission over England

of two of them before becoming entangled with their escorts. In the next few minutes, four merchant ships were sunk by the Stukas and another seven badly damaged. After 20 minutes, the Luftwaffe aircraft found themselves low on fuel and headed home. They had lost three Ju 87s, three Bf 109s and one Bf 110. Two Hurricanes had been shot down, both from 238 Squadron. The Luftwaffe returned at 4pm, with 80 Ju 87s dive bombing the convoy again with an aerial cover provided by 68 fighters. Hurricanes of 43 and 145 Squadron tried to fight them off again, and the squadrons each lost three of their aircraft. Three more Stukas were shot down, and a further two Bf 109s. Peewit had started out with 21 merchant ships. Only four turned up in harbour with no damage. That day – the 8th – cost the Luftwaffe 31 aircraft. The RAF in turn lost 19 planes but twelve of their pilots were killed.

The sheer size of the aerial engagement had another effect. It convinced the RAF that the Luftwaffe were now prepared to attack in ever greater numbers with the intent of forcing a final showdown. British Intelligence was picking up encoded signals between German High Command and the Luftwaffe. Having broken the code, the British commanders read with some trepidation messages such as

'FROM REICHSMARSCHALL GOERING.............. TO ALL UNITS OF LUFTFLOTTES 2, 3 & 5. OPERATION ADLER. WITHIN A SHORT PERIOD YOU WILL WIPE THE BRITISH ROYAL AIR FORCE FROM THE SKY..........HEIL HITLER.'

On 8 August, Goering was indeed planning for a final battle. He had summoned his top commanders to his palatial rural retreat – Karinhall – and, as he and his men played with Goering's prized toy train set, they worked out their plans for the 'Attack of the Eagles' – Adlerangriff, to be commenced with a first day's assault known as Adlertag (Eagle Day). If the RAF would not come out to fight en masse, the Luftwaffe would go to them. Kanalkampf was over. It was time to hit radar facilities, airfields and aircraft production plants. The RAF simply could not afford to lose these. They would have to come up and fight to protect them. Goering now believed the RAF could be smashed in just four decisive days.

Adlerangriff was planned to begin on 10 August but postponed due to violent thunderstorms stretching from Northern France across the Channel into Southern England. Virtually nothing flew. As the weather cleared somewhat on the morning of the 11th, numerous small scale dogfights took place. 74 Squadron was entangled in a fight with Bf 109s on the way to intercept a raid on Dover, and 64 Squadron Spitfires disposed of two Bf 109s over Sussex.

A little after 10am the radar station at Ventnor on the Isle of Wight, reported a huge assembly of enemy aircraft over the Cherbourg Peninsula. Elements of 1, 87, 145, 152, 213 and 238 Squadrons were scrambled to meet it and to join the Spitfires of 609 Squadron who were already up on patrol. What they found as they closed with the enemy was nothing less than the largest single air raid launched against Britain so far – a massed flotilla of 165 aircraft comprising 54 Ju 88s, 20 He 111s, 30 Bf 109s and 61 Bf 110s. The RAF fighters and the German fleet collided all along the Dorset coast between Weymouth and Swanage. It proved to be a brutal wake up call for both sides. By the end of the day, the Luftwaffe had lost 38 aircraft including 15 Bf 109s and 10 Bf 110s. The RAF lost 6 Spitfires and 21 Hurricanes, with an unusually high number of pilot fatalities. Large numbers of bombers had managed to get through while the British interceptors were entangled with the German escorts and they caused significant damage to facilities in Weymouth as well as to the Portland naval base.

On 12 August, the Luftwaffe went after Britain's radar defences. As Bf 109s flew diversionary sorties over England, other warplanes went after the radar. Sixteen bomb-carrying Bf 110s hit the Home Chain Low Station at Dover, before attacking the one at Rye and then moving on to Pevensey. All three were temporarily knocked out. A fourth attack at the Dunkirk station near Canterbury failed. To test the effectiveness of their raids, the Luftwaffe then directed Ju 88s against the RAF forward stations at Lympne near Folkestone and Hawkinge. Hawkinge came off worst. Two hangars were hit and four fighters destroyed on the ground.

Also trying to take advantage of the radar blindness, 120 Bf 110s, 25 Bf 109s and 100 Ju 88s headed for Britain, but they were picked up by an undamaged radar installation at Poling. Ten Spitfires and 48 Hurricanes were sent up to meet them. They were too late to prevent a ferocious attack against Portsmouth by 70 of the Ju 88s and the Royal Dockyards and the railway station suffered considerable damage. The anti-aircraft barrage generated by the guns of Portsmouth brought down two raiders but actually blocked the RAF fighters from closing with the bombers as they ravaged the town. Instead, the fighters pounced as the raiders left, blowing the lead Ju 88 out of the sky over Bognor. While this was happening, more Ju 88s went after the radar station at Ventnor on the Isle of Wight and effectively flattened it. In the early afternoon, Manston aerodrome in Kent was hit by a combined force of Bf 110s and Dorniers, just as a section of 65 Squadron were taxiing to take off on patrol. 175 bombs rained down on them.

This was what Dowding had been dreading. The Luftwaffe had now quite obviously switched to targeting his airfields and the all-important

Junkers Ju87 'Stuka' dive bombers start their attack on an RAF radar station in July 1940 radar stations. Worse, there was a severe breakdown in morale at Manston following the air raid. Many of the ground staff had fled into underground shelters and were now refusing to come out. They would stay there for days, while 600 Squadron pilots had to do their own refuelling and rearming between sorties – and locals wandered on to the near deserted aerodrome to loot it. One RAF officer had to physically restrain a brother officer who had gone to the shelters and was threatening to shoot dead the first man who refused to come out when ordered. Another officer had to be disarmed by the base chaplain.

13 August was the day Goering had designated as Adlertag - Eagle Day. He had had visions of vast, disciplined formations of bombers flying in perfect sunshine to blitz England while masses of fighters flew escort high above them, diving out of the sun to savage any RAF interceptors. Unfortunately for him, the day broke with thick low cloud and fog. He had no desire to postpone Adlertag yet again – and so decided to compromise and temporarily hold all operations until 2pm when his weathermen assured him conditions would improve.

The postponement caused chaos however as not every Luftwaffe base received the orders. 74 Dorniers took off by accident and although their Bf 110 escorts tried to warn them off by performing bizarre aerial manoeuvres (There was no radio transmission between fighters and bombers), they continued undaunted. Over England, the formation split. Part headed for Sheerness naval base and the other for Eastchurch aerodrome, where they destroyed five Blenheims of RAF Coastal Command. Returning, they were intercepted by Hurricanes from 111 and 151 squadrons and five bombers were shot down. The Dornier raid by Kampfgeschwader 2 – which Luftflotte commander Kesselring had to apologise for in person - was just one of several that were not successfully called off that morning. Another early morning raid saw some Bf 110 escorts turn up over Portland for escort duty but without their bombers. They lost five aircraft in six minutes to the combined guns of three squadrons of 10 and 11 Groups acting in a rare example of a 'Big Wing'.

By 1pm, the word had spread that Adlertag was now on. The Germans threw their largest attack formation so far into the air. Leading the charge were 30 Bf 109s with 52 Stukas immediately behind and another formation of Bf 109 escorts to the rear. To the east flew 120 Ju 88s and 30 Bf 110s. To the West were 27 Stukas. Advanced parties of Bf 109s swept over Portland, acting as bait and hoping to draw away RAF fighter formations but didn't succeed. Instead, 80 Hurricanes and Spitfires rose up to meet the main formation.

Luftwaffe bombers punched their way through to Southampton docks causing widespread damage, while 40 Ju 88s were driven away from Portland by persistent fighter defences and lost three of their Bf 110 escorts in the process. Stukas forming up to attack Middle Wallop took too long in their preparations for attack and their fighter escort – desperately low on fuel – had to leave them. They were then bounced by 609 Squadron Spitfires and lost no less than six aircraft. Other Stuka attacks failed when the crews became disorientated and either ditched their bombs or attacked entirely the wrong targets.

A later Stuka attack at 5pm, did catch Detling Aerodrome, a Coastal Command air base, completely by surprise. Bf 109 fighter escorts roared down and strafed the airfield before the dive bombers went in. The effect was devastating. Every hangar was destroyed, the CO killed along with another 66 personnel and 22 aircraft were caught and destroyed on the ground.

That night, Luftwaffe bombers attacked targets as far apart as Belfast, Norwich, Swansea, Aberdeen and Liverpool. The Short's aircraft factory in Belfast was badly hit and five new Stirling bombers destroyed. A Spitfire factory at Castle Bromwich near Birmingham also received severe damage.

The Luftwaffe ended the day estimating that they had destroyed 84 Spitfires and Hurricanes. They were wrong. In reality, they had only claimed 13 RAF fighters and all but three of the pilots shot down had survived. In turn, the RAF thought they had accounted for some 64 Luftwaffe fighters and bombers. The real figure was 47. In numbers terms, Adlertag had turned out to be – if anything – a victory for the RAF, but no-one knew it at the time

Goering wanted to keep the pressure up on the following day but was confounded by more poor weather conditions. There were however still several major clashes during the day. At lunchtime, aircraft from 32, 65 and 610 Squadrons met 90 Bf 109s and 80 Ju 87s over Dover. A massive dogfight ensued, during which seven RAF fighters were shot down for the loss of 3 Stukas and 2 Bf 109s. Caught up in the fighting, RAF fighters were not able to shield Manston Aerodrome from yet another raid by Bf 110s, who succeed in destroying four hangars and three Blenheims on the ground. At 6pm, a lone Ju 88 succeeded in getting through to Middle Wallop, home of 609 Squadron, where it destroyed a hangar full of Spitfires. Another Spitfire on lone patrol took care of the Ju 88 as it finished its bombing run.

By 15 August, Goering had realised fully that Adlertag had not been the success he had been counting on – or the one he had promised the Fuhrer. Entertaining senior commanders at his home, he acknowledged the widespread discontent senior Luftwaffe officers were feeling over the

relatively poor performances of the Bf 110 and Ju 87 Stukas. Goering tried to keep the Ju 87 in action by suggesting that they be escorted by three separate flights of fighters – one to act as a decoy, one to dive alongside the bombers and one to fly high altitude coverage. No one thought it practical. At the same meeting, Goering also ordered that no bomber crew should include more than one officer – a clear indication of how decimated the ranks of Luftwaffe personnel had become. He was not impressed by the results of the attacks on radar stations. Fighter commanders were dismayed by the need for the Bf 109s to fly even tighter escort roles. They thought that their pilots would best achieve the destruction of the RAF by being allowed to go on 'free hunts'.

As Goering spoke, 800 Luftwaffe bombers escorted by 1,000 fighters took off for England, comprising the largest raid of the war so far. Radar picked them up and the RAF scrambled. By 11.30, Ju 87s with a big fighter escort were targeting Hawkinge airfield. The Hurricanes of 501 went after the dive bombers while the Spitfires of 54 Squadron ploughed into the Bf 109s. In the ensuing raid, Hawkinge had one of its hangars destroyed. Nearby Lympne Aerodrome was also hit and both airfields were put out of action for several days. Stukas also attacked the radar stations at Dover, Rye and Foreness, creating a radar blindspot which Bf 109s took advantage of to attack Manston Airfield. They missed the Spitfires of 54 Squadron, who had just refuelled, by minutes, but killed 16 people on the ground as they shot up the airfield.

In a separate attack, 72 He 111s from Luftflotte V, escorted by 20 Bf 110s with long range fuel tanks, set out from Norway to bomb Dundee in the late morning. To save precious fuel on the long journey, all Bf 110s were flying without their rear gunners. The pilots and crews were told that the RAF squadrons in the area had been sent far south to shore up defences on the south coast. The intelligence – as usual - was wrong.

An ingenious diversion by Luftwaffe seaplanes initially drew off RAF interceptors but then the main bomber fleet became lost and accidentally navigated themselves into their own diversion. Eleven Spitfires of 72 Squadron found themselves in an ideal position to intercept. As they saw the Spitfires sweeping in, the He 111s desperately started to jettison their bombs. Two Bf 110s and one He 111 were shot down on the first pass, the Messerschmitts vapourising in the air as bullets hit their long range fuel tanks. Other Bf 110s frantically tried to jettison theirs, but many of the notoriously difficult tanks stayed firmly in place turning the planes into flying fuel bombs. The Spitfires were then replaced by Hurricanes from 605 Squadron, who quickly downed four more bombers. The remaining Luftwaffe aircraft limped home across the North Sea, having lost eight He 111s and a further seven Bf

A formation of Me109s nears the White Cliffs of Dover on the English coast

MAKE SURE
HARNESS LOCKED
BEFORE FLIGHT

110s. One RAF aircraft was lost in the engagement. A further seven Ju 88s from Luftflotte V were lost that same morning, as they launched what was intended to be an unescorted surprise raid on airfields in Yorkshire but were caught out by 12 Spitfires of 616 Squadron and six 73 Squadron Hurricanes from 12 Group. A further three of the raiders were so damaged that they crash-landed at their home base.

The afternoon saw a raid on Martlesham Heath base in Suffolk by Bf 110s and 109s and a massed bombing raid by 88 Dorniers and 130 Bf 109 escorts. Both slipped through due to critical damage to the radar network. The Dorniers inflicted severe damage at Rochester and Eastchurch. More attacks were made against Hawkinge aerodrome, Maidstone, Dover, Middle Wallop, Portland, Worthy Down, Rye and the radar station at Foreness. Responding to the attacks stretched RAF capabilities almost to breaking point. Later in the day, the Luftwaffe would bomb West Malling and – by accident - Croydon. In the latter case, the Bf 110s had been aiming for Kenley. The attack was – technically – an attack on Greater London – something forbidden by Hitler himself. Returning from the raid, the Bf 110s were intercepted by 111 Squadron and lost four aircraft. 32 Squadron joined in and shortly after claimed another three kills.

As night fell, the Germans tallied up their losses. They had flown 2,199 sorties compared with the RAF's 974 and lost seventy five aircraft in a single day, compared with RAF losses of just 30 (including a Blenheim misidentified as a Bf 110 and shot down by friendly fire), with 13 pilots killed. Luftwaffe commanders were particularly shaken by the loss of 28 Bf 110s. The 'Destroyer' was being destroyed. Churchill would call 15 August *'one of the greatest days in history.'* Henceforth, the Germans would refer to it as der schwarze Donnerstag. Black Thursday.

Despite their formidable losses, the Luftwaffe returned in force the next day. A late morning raid by Dorniers got through to West Malling aerodrome and inflicted enough damage to put it out of action for four days. As the first raiders returned home, British radar picked up three much larger formations of enemy aircraft coming in. The first, comprising 24 Dorniers with a Bf 109 escort thought to be targeting Hornchurch aerodrome, was successfully intercepted and chased away by three squadrons of Spitfires. The second formation of 150 aircraft fought its way through to bomb targets including Farnborough and London Docks, with Hurricanes from 111 and 32 Squadrons harassing the bombers as Spitfires from 64, 65 and 266 Squadrons kept their Bf 109 fighter escorts occupied. The third formation, over 100 strong, split into four. Stukas screamed down on Tangmere airfield, destroying 17 aircraft on the ground as below them Spitfire pilots tried to refuel and rearm. More Stukas swooped on Ventnor radar station, causing so much damage that the installation would be out of action for days. Portsmouth Harbour, Lee-on-Solent and Gosport were also bombed.

Three more raids followed in the late afternoon and early evening. Two Ju 88s brazenly lowered their wheels over RAF Brize Norton as they came in pretending to be Blenheims. Ground defences held their fire and the bombers got a clear run at the airfield, managing to destroy a total of 46 aircraft on the ground, including 11 Hurricane fighters.

Prime Minister Winston Churchill personally followed the progress of the raids from 11 Group Headquarters at Uxbridge and saw for himself how stretched fighter defences had become. At one point in the day every single fighter squadron in the Group had been committed – and yet more German raiders were inbound according to the radar. Squadrons were being called upon to fly four or even five separate combat missions over the course of a single day, racing home to refuel and rearm between sorties. Losses inevitably mounted during the day and finally stood at 20 fighters by the time Churchill left Uxbridge. He sat in his staff car, visibly shaken, and demanded silence from his Chief of Staff, General Hastings 'Pug' Ismay. Finally, he managed to sum up his feelings, saying *'Never in the field of human conflict has so much been owed by so many to so few'.*

Neither side could sustain this intense level of combat for much longer. The 'Few' were getting fewer – 78 RAF pilots had been killed in just eight days. On the other side of the Channel, the Luftwaffe had lost almost fifty aircraft over the course of that Friday alone. Saturday 17 August was quiet – so quiet that some radar operators were scared their systems had gone *'on the fritz'.* RAF ground crews took the opportunity presented by the lull in the fighting to effect vital repairs on the airfields. Pilots rested on what one described as a *'heavenly day'*. They read the papers, played a little football in the bright sunshine and celebrated just being alive in the pub come evening. It wasn't to last.

On Sunday 18 August the Luftwaffe came again – and in almost overwhelming force. By lunchtime, radar had picked up huge German formations assembling across the Channel. Every single Squadron in 11 Group was put on alert. The fighting started badly, with Bf 109s ambushing 501 Squadron over Canterbury and shooting down four Hurricanes. Dorniers, flying at almost treetop height, surprised the defences at Biggin Hill but were then set upon by the Hurricanes of 32 and 610 Squadron as they accidentally rained bombs down on a local golf course. Only two of the Do 17s made it home to France. More low flying Dorniers struck Kenley, dropping over a hundred bombs and destroying ten Hurricanes on the ground while putting every hangar

Sergeant pilot in the cockpit of his Spitfire after returning from a sortie

out of action. West Malling and Croydon were also hit.

By 2pm, over 100 Stukas were primed for attack along the South Coast. 22 of them hit Gosport as their Bf 109 escorts tangled with the Spitfires of 234 Squadron and came off worst. Two hangars were destroyed and four aircraft blown to pieces on the ground. The rest of the Stukas targeted Ford, Poling radar station and Thorney Island. Ford was hit particularly hard. The hangars there were hit as well as the fuel storage area. Fourteen aircraft were caught and destroyed on the ground. The fuel dump and more hangars were hit at Thorney Island. But the Stukas didn't have everything their own way – no less than sixteen were shot down during that single raid. The aircraft was rapidly withdrawn from any more widespread use during the Battle of Britain.

Shortly after 5pm, a huge German raiding party from Luftflotte II headed for Hornchurch, comprising 52 He 111s and 58 Dorniers, escorted by 140 Bf 109s and 110s. 32, 54, 56 and 72 Squadrons went up to meet them. The Bf 110s moved to intercept the RAF fighters but they were still flying at little more than 110 mph (to stay beside the slower bombers). Seven Bf 110s fell to the guns of 54 and 56 Squadron in rapid order. More would be lost as the raiders turned back due to increasingly bad weather and poor visibility.

As the last German aircraft touched down on their bases, it became apparent that the RAF had won the day. It was believed that 140 Luftwaffe aircraft had been accounted for. The truth was closer to 70. The RAF for their part had lost just over 30 planes in combat, not counting those destroyed on the ground. Only 10 pilots had been killed.

Goering was incandescent with fury. He called his fighter pilots cowards and sacked some of his officers, replacing them with men he felt had more of a killer instinct. He also ordered closer escort flying, a Bf 109 escort for the struggling Bf 110s at all times and an end to all Stuka operations in the theatre.

The RAF were also trying to adjust their tactics. Pilots were told not to engage over the Channel if at all possible – and to avoid fighting formations of German fighters which were not flying bomber escort. From Bentley Priory, Dowding was doing everything he could to beg, steal or borrow pilots. He got 33 from the Army and 20 ex-Fairey Battle bomber pilots from Bomber Command and kept hunting high and low.

On the airfields now, the pilots were facing near-exhaustion. They could be called upon to fly possibly five combat sorties every single day – and flying seven sorties was far from unheard of. They had to be on call from 3am every single morning. The pilots of 32 Squadron at Biggin Hill took to sleeping out under the wings of their Hurricanes using their parachutes as pillows, while 151 Squadron pilots at Rochford took to sleeping in the cockpits of their already fuelled up and armed fighters. One Spitfire pilot made a perfect landing at his home airfield – only to be discovered asleep at the stick. Shamefully, the cooks on one Dorset airbase declared that they were no longer prepared to get up early to cook the pilots their breakfasts – and so Squadron Leader George Darley of 609 Squadron simply got up and cooked his men breakfast in their place. (The cooks then complained the squadron leader had left them with too much washing up). There were a small number of raids over the next five days as both sides struggled to fight on despite their exhaustion and the damage they had endured.

It was not until Saturday 24 August that the Germans returned with any real force. It was a beautifully clear day over the Channel and South East England – perfect flying weather – and the Luftwaffe would take full advantage. Over the course of the day, they sent more than 500 aircraft over the Channel in six concerted waves.

The first came shortly before 9am – a combined force of 40 Do 17s and Ju 88s escorted by 66 Bf 109s. 610 and 54 Squadron Spitfires hit them hard, breaking them up over Dover and forcing the raiders to retreat homewards. Another raid comprising Ju 88s and Bf 109s was also intercepted and broken up shortly after.

264 Squadron flying Boulton Paul Defiants out of Manston suffered particularly badly that day. When the airfield came under attack from Ju 88s, Defiants racing to take off during the first raid were bounced and three shot down by bomber escorts. The survivors put in at Hornchurch only to be given the order to scramble again as that airfield came under attack. Two more Defiants collided while taxiing to take off and a further aircraft was shot down. Manston was hit twice that day and the decision was finally taken to partly suspend operations there. It was just too vulnerable. North Weald was also hit, despite a successful interception of the bomber fleet by 151 and 111 Squadrons.

To the West, Ju 88s and Bf 110s hit Portsmouth in mid-afternoon and raiders returned by night looking for the Thames Haven oil storage depot and the Short's aircraft factory in Rochester. Navigation proved a problem though and ten aircraft dropped their bombs over London, starting fires from Bethnal Green to Oxford Street. Nine Londoners died. Bombing London was strictly forbidden by Hitler and when Goering found out what had happened he threatened to transfer the guilty crews straight into the infantry. The unintended bombing of civilian areas of London was an accident just waiting to happen. Hitting any target by night was supremely difficult. One Luftwaffe raid on Liverpool, for example, dropped their bombs so far from the target

Heinkel He-111 begins its bombing run over the English countryside

The big raid came when we were all having lunch in the mess and suddenly the tannoy went absolutely mad '616 Squadron scramble, 616 Squadron scramble!' We all dashed out from lunch, grabbed whatever transport we could get hold of and all took off in all sorts of directions, more or less formed up once we'd got airborne and we were vectored on to an enormous raid of about 60 or 70 German bombers. I had never seen so many aircraft in the air before. There were so many and, better still, they were unescorted because they'd come from Norway and the fighter escort had to turn back when they reached the British shores otherwise they wouldn't have enough fuel to get home so they were completely unescorted. They were flying in very close formation and even I couldn't miss them and managed to shoot at three in the short space of time before my ammo ran out.

WILLIAM WALKER, 616 SQUADRON

A brief respite for hard pressed fighter pilots at Hawkinge airfield on the Kent coast

A formation of Heinkel He111s flying over the English countryside

that, next morning, British intelligence officers were left totally baffled as to what they could have possibly been aiming at. The bombing of London, however, was to have huge consequences – and change the direction of the entire Battle of Britain.

Come Sunday, almost 100 Ju 88s with a large scale Bf 109 and 110 escort headed across the Channel and split into three over Weymouth. Part of the formation hit Weymouth itself while the other two formations went for Portland and RAF Warmwell. A later raid comprising Dorniers and Bf 109s was intercepted over Dover.

Monday 26 August saw 150 Luftwaffe aircraft sweep over the south coast by late morning. He 111s bombed Folkestone while 616 Squadron suffered severe losses after their Spitfires were ambushed by as many as 80 Bf 109s. They were lucky to lose only four aircraft and two pilots. The Boulton Paul Defiants of 264 Squadron also suffered more heavy losses as they tried to help intercept the main bomber formation. It was virtually the end of the squadron as a fighting unit. They would only fight once more. More raids followed and the Free Czechs of 310 Squadron 12 Group out of Duxford found themselves in combat for the first time. Their aggression accounted for two Dorniers and a Bf 110, but the Squadron in turn lost three Hurricanes. All three Czech pilots survived to fight again. Throughout the day as the bomber formations tried to push further northward, they often found themselves minus their escorts as the furious dogfighting quickly used up the fighters' relatively meagre fuel supplies. No fighter escort meant greater losses for the bomber formations and, increasingly, they would just dump their bombs and head for home. The day ended with the Luftwaffe having lost some 67 aircraft to the RAF's 27. The night saw bomber raids against Birmingham, Bournemouth, Plymouth and Coventry.

After a lull in the fighting due to bad weather, the Luftwaffe struck again early on the morning of Wednesday 28 August. He 111s went for Rochford and Dorniers for Eastchurch. 79 Squadron Hurricanes and 264 Squadron Defiants intercepted the Rochford raid but the Defiants found themselves up against the vastly superior Bf 109s and four more were shot down. They would now be withdrawn from daylight fighting. Neither raid had much effect - and neither did a second raid on Rochford a few hours later. 4pm saw 54, 56, 85, 151 and 603 Squadrons vectored to intercept what was thought to be a large bomber formation. It turned out to be a mass of Bf 109s and 110s just spoiling for a fight. They got it. 17 RAF fighters were lost over the course of the day's events. By night, 150 Luftwaffe bombers delivered the first mass bombing raid – against Liverpool – with minimal effect while smaller raids were experienced in seven other towns and cities including Birmingham, Bristol, Manchester and Derby.

The Luftwaffe continued its mass fighter missions on the afternoon of 29 August. A small formation of decoy He 111s were sent over Beachy Head with 150 Bf 110s and over 500 Bf 109s just waiting for the RAF fighters when they appeared. With 13 Squadrons in the air ready to fight, the RAF controllers worked desperately to keep their squadrons away from the trap and largely succeeded.

Frustrated by their failure to lure the RAF into the trap, the Luftwaffe threw almost everything they had at South East England on Friday 30 August. Three waves of enemy aircraft swept in. The first was comprised

Pilots of 504 Squadron scramble for their Hurricanes at Hendon aerodrome

65 Squadron pilot at Hornchurch in his Spitfire

entirely of fighters looking for a dogfight. The second, half an hour later, mixed 70 He 111 and Do 17 bombers with 90 fighter escorts. They were hit first by 11 Hurricanes of 85 Squadron which helped to break up their formation. Two Bf 110s were shot down for the loss of one Hurricane and 43, 79 and 603 Squadron hit the formation as it continued towards Ashford.

Rolling in behind this formation was yet another Luftwaffe fleet. Radar operators were stunned to see their screens almost filled with aircraft signals. The skies over South East England were packed with aircraft formations and wheeling dogfights. By noon everything 11 Group had was in the air. Park turned to his counterpart, Leigh-Mallory, to supply 12 Group squadrons in protection of Kenley and Biggin Hill aerodromes. Ignoring their orders, the pilots of 12 Group went off in search of prey – leaving the airfields wide open to attack.

Three more waves of Luftwaffe fighters and bombers joined the melee in the early afternoon. Shoreham, Tangmere and Kenley airfields were all bombed by Ju 88s. Seven vital radar stations were knocked out by bombing which affected the electricity supply. Between four and six pm 19 more Luftwaffe Gruppen came over, looking for airfields and aircraft factories. The Vauxhall Works at Luton was badly damaged. Ju 88s caught 79 Squadron on the ground at Biggin Hill, destroying three Spitfires and obliterating one of the airfield's four remaining hangars. A badly stretched RAF had flown 1054 combat sorties that day – a total which would turn out to be the highest flown during the entire Battle of Britain. 22 squadrons had flown in the fight and of those it was not uncommon for a squadron to go up on four different occasions. 56 Squadron flew seven times during the course of the day.

The Luftwaffe started early on the morning of 31 August, with a force of Bf 109s spoiling for a fight. RAF fighter command tried to avoid them but not before they had succeeded in chewing up 1 Squadron and shooting down three fighters. Shortly after, a large formation of Luftwaffe bombers and Bf 110s split up over the Thames Estuary and headed off for RAF airfields. North Weald and Debden were particularly badly hit. Later formations went for Croydon and Biggin Hill. 85 Squadron managed to scramble just as the raiders appeared over Croydon but Biggin Hill was hit worse, losing two more hangars and two parked Spitfires to a low level attack. Hornchurch was also hit, just as its Spitfires were trying to scramble. Later raids damaged both Biggin Hill and Hornchurch once again and there were strikes against a number of radar stations.

The Luftwaffe were successfully refining their tactics. The hits on the airfields were starting to cripple the fighter squadrons on the ground, disrupting them and depriving them of essential facilities. At the same time, the massed fighter escorts were proving effective cover for the bombers, whether the fighter pilots liked it or not. On 31 August the Luftwaffe still lost 39 aircraft – but the RAF had lost 37 of their own, with 13 pilots killed.

The battle was now turning in favour of the Germans...

Day in the Life

Every day was the same but every day was different. Different airfields, different leaders and different squadrons but the enemy was always the same. The pilots all remember different things about their daily routine.

Well you were often told you were going to be up at dawn so you actually got up in the dark and you went straight down, having had a quick breakfast, down to your dispersal and you sat there waiting for things to happen. Sometimes if we were told there was no activity going on we would wander up and go to the ops room and sit around looking to see what was happening or we would just stay down at dispersal and have a quick nap. There were lots of books and magazines to read and we often talked to the airmen and found out what they had been doing. A lot of very good chaps had been conscripted in and they were always very keen to talk to the pilots and we would pass the day that way. It was pretty exhausting and towards the end of the day you were absolutely shattered.

John Ellacombe

Normally you were up at dawn, you were at readiness. You were scrambled to go into quite a large number of enemy aircraft. You were fighting in the skies over Kent and Sussex. You probably didn't have time for breakfast. Some times it was brought round to dispersal, other times after say, a trip, you'd be put to 15 minutes available and you could get in a transport and go off to the mess and get yourself a lunch and then back and I think probably, people say five or six times a day, well I don't know about that. I think a more realistic number is three. I mean by the time you'd got airborne, I mean that was five or six hours in the air, pretty hectic combat, and by the time the aeroplane had got back on the ground, been rearmed, refuelled, checked over, this five or six business I think is a lot of media hype on that. I have done four but I think three trips is probably the average, and two of the big combats, one in the morning and one in the afternoon because the Germans had to refuel, rearm, in between that you'd probably do a convoy escort if there was one going up the east coast or something like that but that was a more normal day I think but certainly you were down at dispersal from early dawn until dusk. Luckily, if things had quietened down, ops used to send us back to 30 minutes which meant we could go back to the mess, have a cup of tea or something and a sit down in comfort.

Geoffrey Wellum

There wasn't such a thing as a typical day in the battle. You'd go to readiness at a prescribed time because they tried to rotate squadrons so that two squadrons on the station were not both being up at dawn and we'd be usually up at first light, out to the dispersal and the aircraft would be warmed up by the ground crew and you would sit around awaiting instructions. And the telephone would ring so you'd always be on the alert, grabbing your helmet ready to run and you'd hear the chap answering the phone, 'No, Corporal Smith's gone to breakfast. He's not here I'm afraid' and he'd put the phone down and we'd all relax and this would happen so frequently we'd say to each other 'God, when this war's over I'm not going to have a damn telephone in my house.' It was frustrating in the extreme and then of course you'd get the real call and the chap would suddenly shout, holding the telephone in his hand '32 Squadron, patrol Ashford, Angels 15' and you'd all rush out, get into your aircraft and the squadron commander led off, then you'd follow as flight commander with your flight and off you'd go to Ashford and probably before you got anywhere near Ashford you'd run into a German formation which was quite startling when you first saw them.

Pete Brothers

Oh yes, oh you sprinted but you didn't run in formation like the newsreels show you, pilots running in formation. You'd be going from different angles. You just got to your aircraft as quickly as possible. Absolutely. You would have your backside kicked, there's no doubt about that. You had to run. On occasions we did sit in the aircraft. We were brought to readiness sitting in your aircraft. We were sitting there with our parachutes on, helmets on and just sitting there and then you'd get the signal to scramble and suddenly a verey pistol would fire a signal, a light would go up, and you'd go off.

Tony Pickering

Well, it depends on what sort of readiness you've got. Our usual readiness was 30 minutes and this meant that people had got their parachutes already on the aircraft - if it was mine it would be hanging off the port wing – I used to keep it on the port tailplane until they put our bloody silly IFF on and I couldn't dangle it over the IFF aerial and so it used to go on the port wing which was just as well as you walk up and under it grab the two straps, pull away, it fell on your back – came round – click click, bent down, strap between your legs, click click and you're finished. 10 seconds and you're on your way back to get in. Most people, like myself, used to go out if we knew we were going to be on readiness between 7 till 12, something like that, put the chute in place, climb up on the wing, when it got icy it got a bit troublesome, that, I tried once four times to get up on the wing and slid off every time but eventually you managed to get your hand over the canopy and press the little button down which meant you could slide the hood back, you were away then. So you climb on board, people adopted various habits after that. Most people did as I did, get their feet inside and sit comfortably on the empty seat, and I mean empty because there was no cushion on it, we relied on the parachute for that and our helmet was hung, against all regulations, over the bloody mirror sight and the RT lead was plugged into the connection on the front of the seat and the oxygen tube was hung on a loop into the little connector on the side of the cockpit just behind the right hand side of the dashboard. I stuffed my gloves back behind the gunsight and just dragged them out when we got on board. We then sat and prepared the aircraft, made sure the brakes were on and operated them and read the readings on the dial to make sure they were operating correctly and were hard on. We checked the throttle, that it was not locked hard, and set it to where we wanted it to be, about half an inch open and then locked it. The propeller, we made sure that was in the starting position and there were various other bits and pieces to make sure the aircraft was ready for immediate take off and then we got out, shut the hood again and went over to the hut.

Dennis David

There was a certain routine when we were down at Hornchurch. If the phone rang once they were talking to somebody in the mess. If it rang twice it was for you and you were going to be scrambled. If it rang three times it was for the other squadron. So when you were sitting down and the phone suddenly rang you said 'Once...will it stop?' 'Twice...is that us?' 'Thank God its a third time'. An extraordinary situation of tenseness. Were we going to be scrambled or weren't we? And that was the phone but again you never knew when the phone rang what was going to happen. It was a situation where nerves began to play quite a part.

John Ellacombe

Of course you could get airborne quickly. At Croydon we'd take off as a squadron because it was a grass airfield and you could get all 12 aeroplanes lined up right across the airfield, a wonderful sight, and all 12 Hurricanes would get airborne at the same time, and then form up into your four vics and climb together.

Bob Foster

Well there's a lot of talking going on. Of course we had Joe Pegg's bloody gramophone. 'She had to go and lose it at the Astor', that was Joe Pegg's favourite. It was on the go incessantly. It was a wind up type, used to play about two records before it needed winding again. They'd got a bulletin board. We used to get a day off a week when we used to disappear into Newcastle for a day and get back early morning the next day and we used to bring back any magazine or picture we could which would go on this board and had some of the most atrocious photographs you'd ever seen. In fact, if we got visitors, say from Army cadets or RAF cadets, who's officers had brought their wives up, Joe Pegg used to make an immediate dash for the wife and say 'Come and see our bulletin board'. What they thought of these pictures I don't know. There was an awful lot of talking going on. Some people read but I couldn't be bothered to read as there was so much going on besides. You could wander outside and watch what's going on. Things of interest all the time because we had about 30 odd accidents up there, stupid accidents. I think I had two, or maybe three, and there were interesting people who used to come in other aircraft. There was the day a Beaufighter landed and Joe Pegg walked across to ask the pilot for his opinion on the weather, as it had been pretty bloody awful, we had a heavy sea fog roll in, he was quite pleased he had done when she took her helmet off, it was a woman pilot, and of course she didn't have radio on board.

David Denchfield

When we were at North Weald especially we used to get a lot of information from sector ops on the state of the enemy because the enemy was taking off in northern France and of course the bombers used to take about an hour to get the height so they would gradually form up over northern France or Belgium and it would appear on our radar screens, or our sector radar screens, and we used to get that information and that was really the most apprehensive part of our flight. The fighters took off a little later because they didn't have to form up before they came across to England so it was the period before the fighting, when we were having these messages passed to us of what was happening 20, 30, 40, 50, 100+, 150+, my God and there are only 12 of us, where do we start? and eventually we'd be scrambled. Now as soon as we were scrambled, and the fighting started you didn't give it a thought, or at least I didn't give it a thought. I was too busy avoiding the blokes flying next to me and looking for the enemy and getting out of the way of the ack ack, as the ack ack used to come up in sheets all over the place and as often as not we'd be hit by our own ack ack just as often as we were hit by the enemy. No, the actual business of fighting is the easiest part of it. Depends whether you were clobbered by the enemy return fire or enemy fighter but you probably wouldn't be feeling so good about it then but generally speaking the apprehensive part was the period before the fighting.

Tom Neil

We even got caught out during the Battle of Britain, at Biggin Hill, the clouds were on the ground and they said that the Meteorological chap said it was going to stay there so they told us we were stood down for the day. That was the first mistake. We were very new, it was very early on and instead of getting the hell off the station and out of the way we stayed in the bar drinking and suddenly at two o'clock, despite the Met forecast the weather cleared and not only were we brought to readiness we were scrambled in quick time and I remember I was well and truly under the alcohol stimulus, flying along thinking 'Well what should I do? Yes, turn the gun button on to fire, yes, so that's ready. Yes, reflector sight, I'd better switch the sight on. Yes' but it was amazing, as soon as you got in contact with the enemy the amount of adrenalin, you were stone cold sober in seconds with sheer fright.

Pete Brothers

Well we were all very cheerful chaps. We used to go in the bar and chat and have a drink and then when you were desperately tired you'd go to bed. What we did at North Weald, Victor Beamish made us, every third day or fourth day, you would get off the station. We used to nip down to London and go to some of the old pubs or places we had known or visit your friends or go into Ongar where we had pals and it was a very nice pub there. We'd go and have a lunch and chat to people but Victor Beamish wanted you to get away every fourth day so that was one way we used to try and reduce the strain.

John Ellacombe

Well we used to go down to the local pub because by that time the evenings were coming in. We were a day fighter squadron, we were not equipped to fly as night fighters. One or two of the more senior pilots did try and do this but it was never successful. One or two of the very senior pilots would be sent off at night time in Hurricanes to try and attack the bombers but it was done rarely because they were just not equipped. They had no radar or anything like that. They just had to look out of a Hurricane and try and find the bombers. It just didn't work. It was not successful. So we invariably would go out as small groups of sergeants together and the officers together but the sergeants had the advantage over the officers. I've always mentioned this before to people. We as sergeants were allowed to mix with the WAAF girls, these young girls of 18 and 19 years of age. The officers were not allowed to do it. They were very strict. Officers were not allowed to mix with the WAAFs. So we, the few sergeant pilots in the squadron, had the pick of girls on the station. I think that we, as young men of 18 and 19 years of age respected these girls. We'd been taught by our parents to respect girls and we were young lads and they respected us. They were lovely girls and I've always admired those girls because they were well brought up, well educated and quite frankly they behaved themselves and we, to a large extent, behaved ourselves. Quite frankly the evenings we spent with them were really enjoyable and I've never forgotten them. We had some lovely times together, walking back from the pub at about 10.30 at night back to the aerodrome, a mile, OK we used to stop and have a cuddle or something like that but nevertheless

RAF bomber crew do final checks before an operation to Berlin *they were nice girls but they were the ones who suffered, we didn't, and those girls stuck it out. There were a lot killed at Biggin, lot of WAAFs killed at Biggin. Certainly these girls were very brave. Always admired them. They were the ones who got bombed. We didn't. We took off but these young girls of 18 and 19 years of age were on the aerodrome, later on we moved to Kenley and they got bombed. There weren't any bombs dropped at Gravesend but when we moved at the beginning of September to Kenley, the Royal Air Force permanent station, the WAAFs there looked after us and they looked after us very well.*

TONY PICKERING

During the whole time one was at readiness you were tired. You were taken off readiness at about half past nine or ten at night and then you went to the mess and you had a beer or two in the mess and then it was bed so that you didn't probably get to bed until half past ten or eleven and at half past three you were woken up again. The one thing you remembered was you were always tired during those days.

WILLIAM WALKER

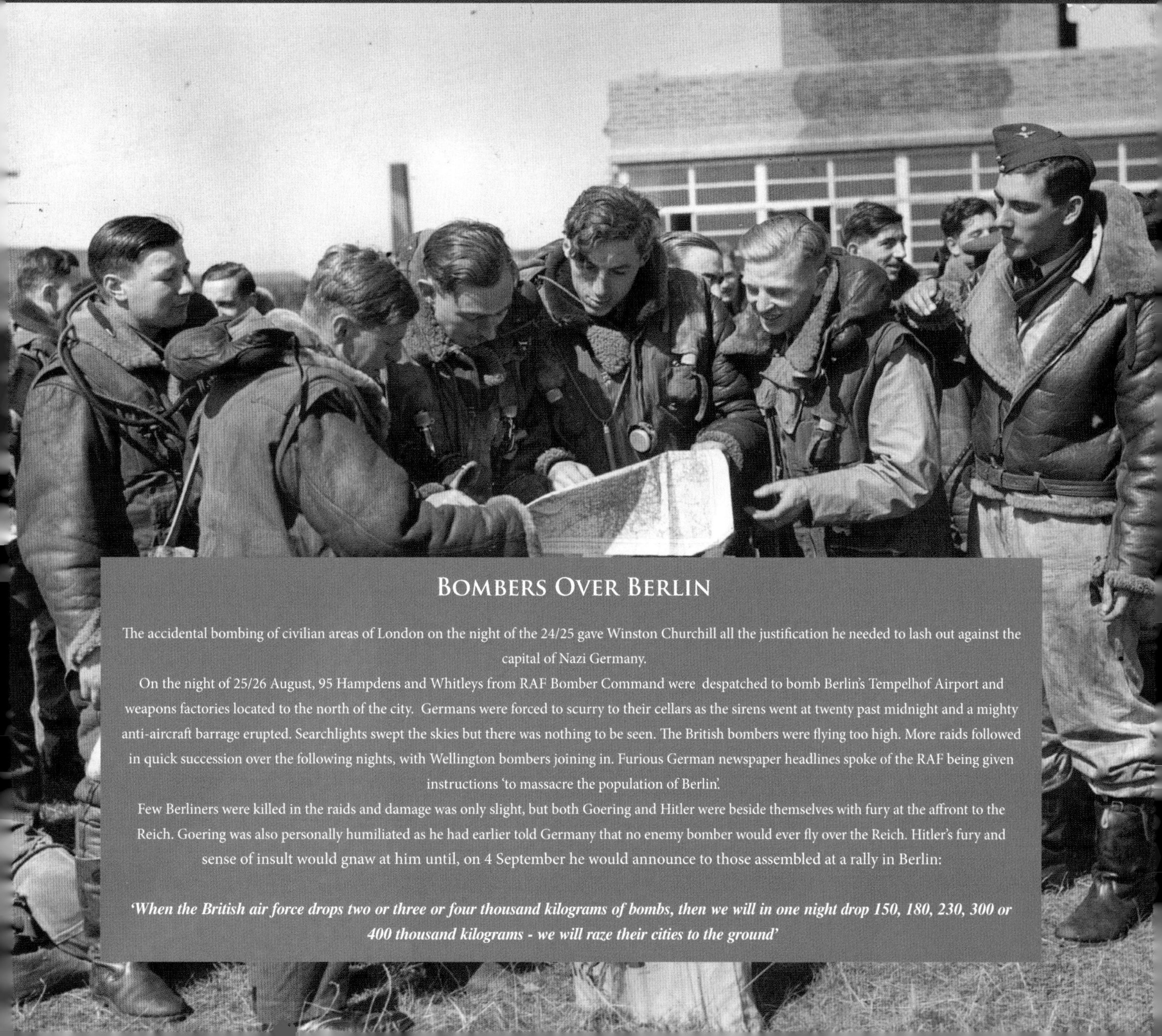

BOMBERS OVER BERLIN

The accidental bombing of civilian areas of London on the night of the 24/25 gave Winston Churchill all the justification he needed to lash out against the capital of Nazi Germany.

On the night of 25/26 August, 95 Hampdens and Whitleys from RAF Bomber Command were despatched to bomb Berlin's Tempelhof Airport and weapons factories located to the north of the city. Germans were forced to scurry to their cellars as the sirens went at twenty past midnight and a mighty anti-aircraft barrage erupted. Searchlights swept the skies but there was nothing to be seen. The British bombers were flying too high. More raids followed in quick succession over the following nights, with Wellington bombers joining in. Furious German newspaper headlines spoke of the RAF being given instructions 'to massacre the population of Berlin'.

Few Berliners were killed in the raids and damage was only slight, but both Goering and Hitler were beside themselves with fury at the affront to the Reich. Goering was also personally humiliated as he had earlier told Germany that no enemy bomber would ever fly over the Reich. Hitler's fury and sense of insult would gnaw at him until, on 4 September he would announce to those assembled at a rally in Berlin:

'When the British air force drops two or three or four thousand kilograms of bombs, then we will in one night drop 150, 180, 230, 300 or 400 thousand kilograms - we will raze their cities to the ground'

DIRECTIVE 17

By the end of July 1940, it had become obvious to Adolf Hitler that the tactic of trying to entice the RAF out to fight in large numbers over the Channel was not yielding sufficiently fast nor favourable results. His commanders were urging him to postpone any thoughts of invasion until May 1941 but Hitler wanted this matter settled now. By 1941 he wanted to be waging war with the Soviets. He compromised. The invasion would be pushed back to September 1940 – and every effort would be made to make it feasible. Consequently, on 1 August, he issued Directive 17 which called for the intensification of 'air and sea warfare against the English homeland'.

First and foremost, he ordered:

'The German Air Force is to overpower the English Air Force with all the forces at its command, in the shortest time possible. The attacks are to be directed primarily against flying units, their ground installations, and their supply organizations, but also against the aircraft industry, including that manufacturing anti-aircraft equipment'

ATTACKS ON CONVOYS WERE DE-PRIORITISED.

That same day, a fleet of 30 He 111s bombed the Boulton Paul aircraft factory in Norwich and other bombers dropped masses of leaflets featuring a message from Hitler – his *'Appeal to Reason'*. In it he railed against the Treaty of Versailles, accused the French and British of being warmongers for declaring war against Germany both in 1914 and 1939, claimed that Norwegian, Dutch and Belgian neutrality had really been threatened by Britain and France, boasted that his losses in the war so far had been negligible and he had more than sufficient forces at his disposal to seize Britain. However he said, he regretted that Britain and Germany were not friends and ended with an appeal.

'In this hour I feel it to be my duty before my own conscience to appeal once more to reason and common sense, in Great Britain as much as elsewhere. I consider myself in a position to make this appeal since I am not the vanquished begging favours, but the victor speaking in the name of reason. I can see no reason why this war must go on.'

Most of the leaflets fell in the wilds of East Anglia and the West Country where sheep and cows were their only audiences. Those that did reach the British public were apparently put to good use as national newspapers quickly published cartoons showing the 'Appeal to Reason' being hung in numerous outdoor toilets by a grateful citizenry.

Luftwaffe spearhead Ju-87 'Stuka' dive bombers in massed formation approaching England

Churchill Names 'The Few'

Inspired – and profoundly moved - by his experience of witnessing a day's combat operations at RAF Uxbridge on 16 August, Churchill had ended the day by saying to his Chief of Staff, General Ismay that *'Never in the field of human conflict has so much been owed by so many to so few'*. It was a phrase he would use again before Parliament on 20 August in one of the most famous speeches ever to be put before the House of Commons. He would say:

'The gratitude of every home in our Island, in our Empire, and indeed throughout the world, except in the abodes of the guilty, goes out to the British airmen who, undaunted by odds, unwearied in their constant challenge and mortal danger, are turning the tide of the world war by their prowess and by their devotion. Never in the field of human conflict was so much owed by so many to so few. All hearts go out to the fighter pilots, whose brilliant actions we see with our own eyes day after day…'

Churchill takes time for a photo with RAF volunteers

FLIGHT LIEUTENANT JAMES NICOLSON

On 16 August, Gosport was attacked by a formation of Ju 88 bombers with an escort of Bf 110s. The raid was intercepted by a flight of three 249 Hurricanes, led by Flight Lieutenant James Nicolson, which were up on patrol. Chasing after a pair of Ju 88s, he was suddenly hit by fire from one of the fighter escorts. Shells slammed into his reverse fuel tank, catching Nicolson's fighter on fire. Smoke and flames rapidly filled his cockpit, and his instrument panel began to melt in front of him. He later described it as *'dripping like treacle'*. Despite this, Nicolson stayed with his aircraft and went after the Bf 110 that had been shooting at him. He successfully shot it down and only then gave thought to bailing out. Blinded by blood in his left eye he threw himself out of his doomed hurricane but – as he tried to pull his ripcord, he found that both his hands were so badly burned that he couldn't get a grip. After plunging more than five hundred feet, he finally succeeded in gripping the ripcord and deploying his chute. Still Nicolson wasn't out of danger. Elements of the local Home Guard started shooting at him as he descended and he was unfortunate enough to be shot in the buttocks. Three months later, Flight Lieutenant Nicolson would be awarded the Victoria Cross for his bravery, the only VC to be issued during the Battle of Britain.

We intercepted another 88. This produced a wonderful story because the aircraft was badly hit and decided it couldn't get home so it turned towards the coast and it landed in Yorkshire. The pilot was killed, and the crew got out into this foreign land called Britain and they couldn't find anybody around so they went towards the nearest farmhouse and the farmer's wife looked out of the window and saw them coming and thought 'My God, we're being invaded' so she rushed out with a pitchfork and attacked these people. These poor men were wounded and not feeling very happy as they'd just been shot down and this crazy woman with a pitchfork attacked them and then of course the following day it appeared in the papers how this very brave woman had tackled the crew. We went to the films to see it on the Movietonenews and were absolutely horrified and astonished to find that it had been credited to a Spitfire squadron up north so we didn't even get the credit for it but the lady got an OBE or MBE having attacked them with a pitchfork.

TOM NEIL, 249 SQUADRON

Downed Pilots

It's estimated that 80% of all pilots and aircrew who ended up in the Channel died. Over land, half of all those who bailed out survived. As the air war moved inland and away from the convoys in August 1940, the RAF found that more and more of their pilots were surviving being shot down. Luftwaffe pilots and crew were now of course at more of a disadvantage. Shot down over the Channel, if they survived the ordeal they had a good chance of being picked up and returned to their units by their own very efficient air-sea rescue service. Being shot down over the British countryside was different. There were no known instances of Luftwaffe personnel bailing out over England and escaping again. The crew of a Heinkel He 111 did avoid being captured for a week after bailing out but were eventually apprehended. Another bomber crew, whose plane came down in Graveney Marsh decided to fight back and got into a shooting match with the soldiers sent to detain them. After some grand posturing and one of the German crewmen being shot in the foot, they eventually surrendered and the opposing sides then retired for a pint together in the local pub. Not all Germans received such a decent welcome. There were known instances of downed Luftwaffe crews being murdered. On 28 August the crew of a Heinkel 111 that came down on the beach at East Wittering in Sussex were all shot dead by soldiers of the Duke of Cornwall's Light Infantry and a Dornier pilot was beaten to death by an angry mob after being shot down over Victoria Station and landing in Kennington.

There are numerous stories of RAF pilots being mistaken for German parachutists and being roughly treated by the civilians who came to capture them. Even VC winner Flight Lieutenant James Nicolson was shot by a member of the Home Guard on his descent, and his life was only saved by a British soldier pointing a gun at the amateurs and keeping them from him until help arrived. Polish and Czech pilots in particular, who tended to speak very little - if any- English were often mistaken for Germans and sometimes badly ill-treated. Shortly after the Blitz began, a Polish fighter pilot landed in Wapping. Already seriously injured, he was unable to identify himself and the mob that gathered beat him to death. (Yet, happily in another case, a Polish fighter pilot bailed out and landed right in front of a pretty young English girl. They were married two months later.)

German airmen, who parachuted from a shot-down Heinkel HE-111 bomber are escorted by the Home Guard in Goodwood, Sussex

SHOOTING DOWN THE ENEMY

Most of the pilots who claimed one 'kill' or more remembered it in a very modest and dispassionate way. They talked of seeing it as shooting the aircraft rather than the pilot and there was obviously a huge amount of concentration involved in those few seconds while they flew straight and level behind the enemy aircraft. One reason why there seems to have been many bullets fired but few aircraft shot down was explained by Tom Neil.

I can only describe it as miserable. We learned later that of all the bullets fired in the Battle of Britain, and indeed later in the war, about 3% of the rounds fired actually hit the target. Putting it another way 97% missed. The gunsight wasn't really very good until we began to get the gyroscopic gunsight which came in late 1944, 1945. In the First World War you had the ring and bead sight which was purely calculating for deflection. The gunsight that we had in the Hurricane and Spitfire, the first Spitfires, believe it or not,was the ring and bead sights, from the First World War but then we had the reflector sight which was really a more up to date presentation of the ring and bead but people couldn't hit anything as a result of deflection shooting to save themselves and the only way to hit anything was to get directly behind the other chap, as close as you possibly could, close your eyes and fire.

Perhaps that shows how good the pilots had to be to actually shoot down an enemy aircraft.

I went up with a Sergeant Harker, I was his number two, he was the more experienced pilot and one of the things I do remember at that time is the radio was very faulty. We had great problems with the radio. When you see films about the Battle of Britain and 11 Group particularly, they were able to talk to each other without any trouble, I never was able to talk to anyone without trouble. You got spasms when it wasn't too bad but on the whole it was very unreliable, the radio was very unreliable. Anyway we went off and as the newcomer to the squadron naturally I didn't get first choice of aeroplane so he was going off and I was supposed to be number two to him but he was getting further and further ahead of me, I just couldn't stay with him but we were in pursuit of a Junkers 88 and he fired at it and some distance in front of me some smoke came out and shortly after that he turned round and decided to go home and I looked at my fuel supply and decided that I'd got enough to go a bit further. We'd both been catching up with the 88, he'd been doing it faster than I, and I came up within firing range and it was going down by this time, he had smoke coming out of him and he was going down, and I fired at him and I think I hit him, some more smoke came out of him. He took a steeper dive and he went into the sea. I didn't claim anything as Sgt Harker had shot it down but in fact Intelligence officers decided I should have a share in the victory so that was my first. My first plus mark was a half victory.

TERENCE KANE

Heinkel 111, Dungeness. It was the first time I was in action. I followed Brian into this mass and it broke away and then below I saw a Heinkel that had obviously left its formation going full bore back towards Dungeness and so I had a go at him and was fortunate enough to get a confirmation. It crashed on Dungeness and that was when I got shot up in 'K' because I was so keen on 'Aren't you a clever boy!' but there was this enormous bang and there was a 109 sitting behind me, very very close indeed. I could see the paint peeling off the leading edge. He must have been no more than, it's terribly easy to exaggerate, but I reckon 30 yards and I remember automatically thumping the Spitfire into the most brutal turn and thinking I'm going to be killed. Then I thought well sod it because I can out turn him. I knew he was on the limit and all the time I kept the Spit on the limit and you knew it was on the limit because, dear aeroplane that it was, before it stalled, in a high speed stall, it would judder, the Spit would judder. Now if you were good you could hold it on that judder, lots of power, stick right back, hard over and the 109 couldn't stay with you and I remember seeing, I'm pretty certain that I didn't imagine it, but they had slats all the way along the leading edge to ease off, they had quite a vicious stall, and they used to come out and I thought 'You're on the limit mate' and if I keep going like this I'm going to be a very difficult target and eventually that's what I did and I got back. In fact I think I might have had two that day because I shot at a Dornier, a jolly good burst it was too.

GEOFFREY WELLUM

Well the strange thing was we'd been attacking Ju88s, bombers, and I got myself nicely positioned behind this Ju88 and he suddenly saw me, I was in a Hurricane, he suddenly saw me, this guy, he knew I was behind him. I don't know whether I gave him a quick burst but he just opened his taps, I'd got my throttle fully open and he went faster than me by at least 50mph. Absolutely amazed me, that did, what type of Ju88 it was I don't know but he just opened his throttles completely and before I could do anything more about it he shot away from me and although I bent my throttle lever over as far as I could get, it was metal and you could push it and get a bit more, I couldn't get near him. But then I saw this 109 coming and I got behind him and shot him down. This 109, I don't think he was trying to attack me, I think he'd been attacked. I think somebody had had a go at him but there was no-one else in the sky so I thought 'Right, just the job' and I got behind him and I got to shoot him down. He was a darn sight slower than the Ju88. He couldn't get away from me. I was able to hold my speed such as I stayed behind him but I couldn't with the Ju88. I've never forgotten that. It's a bit strange. That was a fairly simple case, I must be honest. I think he'd been knocked about by some Spitfires or Hurricanes. Someone had had a go at him but he'd got away. No-one was behind him, nobody was near him, he was all by himself and I got behind him and knocked him down.

TONY PICKERING

We were jumped by some 109s out of the sun. The first we knew about it was a frantic shout 'break, break, break!' which meant you didn't sit around arguing, you just broke and I broke down and the 109s came down on us and shot down a chap called Charles English and damaged somebody else and I went down and pulled out of the dive, looked around and ahead of me was a 109, flying straight and level, heading south and going home. Whether he saw me I don't know but I got straight behind him and shot him down. He could have been one of the ones that attacked us and thought it was all over and done with and was going home. As I said, it didn't matter which side you were on you couldn't afford to relax so that was that occasion, I remember quite well.

BOB FOSTER

The Hurricane guns, there were eight of them, I was unable to pull my guns in to one point. The nearest I could get, wingtips, was 167 yards, I do know that, and they came down to one point and I did this because I reckoned the only way to make a kill was to get really close. On one occasion I shot a Heinkel 111and suddenly there was a burst of oil and I thought I had blown my own engine up but when my fitter got to clean it up afterwards, I landed fairly quickly, they found it was German oil, the Heinkel 111's oil tanks had blown up and come into my aeroplane. That gives you an idea how close we were. That I think gives you the idea that it was an important part of fighting and, of course, a determined attack like that makes the German pilots a bit more scared.

DENNIS DAVID

Wreckage of a Me-109 shot down on 29 August 1940 being displayed for the camera

JOSEF FRANTISEK – THE 'LONE WOLF'

The third highest scoring RAF air ace of the Battle of Britain was a Czech pilot – Sergeant Josef Frantisek. He flew with 303 (Polish) Squadron and is credited with 17 confirmed kills. He achieved this in just 27 days. Originally a fighter pilot with the Czech Air Force, Frantisek escaped to Poland when the Nazis overran his homeland and later fought with the Polish Air Force when Poland was invaded in September 1939. In one famous escapade, he is credited with flying at treetop level over an enemy troop column and dropping hand grenades on them out of his fighter's open cockpit. As Poland fell, he escaped first to Romania and then to France, where he flew for the French Air Force under an assumed name. He is widely credited with shooting down as many as eleven German aircraft before escaping again as France fell, this time to England. Because of 'personal difficulties' with a Czech Officer, he was assigned to the Polish 303 Squadron where he quickly gained the reputation of an ill-disciplined maverick who was pretty dangerous to fly with. Rather than kick him out though, 303's Squadron Leader Kellett decided to let him fly with the squadron as a 'guest'. He'd take off with 303 Squadron but then peel off to fight his own personal war as a 'Lone Wolf'. It was an inspired decision. During September 1940, Frantisek claimed 17 kills (including nine Bf 109 fighters) and won the DFM – the first foreign pilot to be so honoured. His preferred method was to bounce enemy aircraft as they returned from their mission and to close in on his target and blast them from as little as 40 feet away. As Frantisek's kills increased, so did his irrational behaviour. It was clear that he was fatigued to the point of exhaustion as well as being deeply psychologically troubled. He confided in his fellow pilots that he was starting to feel frightened all the time – except when he was flying. On 8 October 1940, when returning home, Frantisek's Hurricane suddenly banked away and slammed into the ground. Frantisek was thrown from his aircraft, broke his neck and died instantly. There were no German aircraft in the area.

It was this Sailor Malan thing. Height is essential, don't hang around in the sky congratulating yourself, never fly straight and level in the combat area, get in, hit the bombers hard and get out again, and keep your eyes open all the time. That's about the basics of the thing and if you did that you stood a better chance of getting away with it. I think a lot of chaps, having attacked, thought well that's it, let's go home and they didn't make it.

BOB FOSTER, 605 SQUADRON

Adolph 'Sailor' Malan

Sailor Malan was the best pilot of the war; a good tactician, an above average pilot and an excellent shot. '

Air Commodore Alan Deere

South African air ace Adolph Malan was a merchant seaman by trade who started his career with the RAF in 1937 because a life at sea wasn't paying enough and he needed to earn more to get married. Because of his background, everyone called him 'Sailor'. He won the DFC for his part in the aerial combat over Dunkirk and became an ace after downing five German aircraft. Malan took command of the Spitfires of 74 Squadron from 8 August 1940, then considered an elite squadron, and on 11 August alone, the Squadron claimed 38 kills. He gained a reputation of being as fierce with his subordinates as he was in the air. He was credited with 27 kills, seven shared and a further three probables by the end of the Battle of Britain.

As well as helping to evolve fighter formation tactics from the 3-aircraft 'Vic' formation to the 4-aircraft Finger Four, Malan also drew up a list of 'tips' for fighter pilots that were shared far and wide throughout Fighter Command:

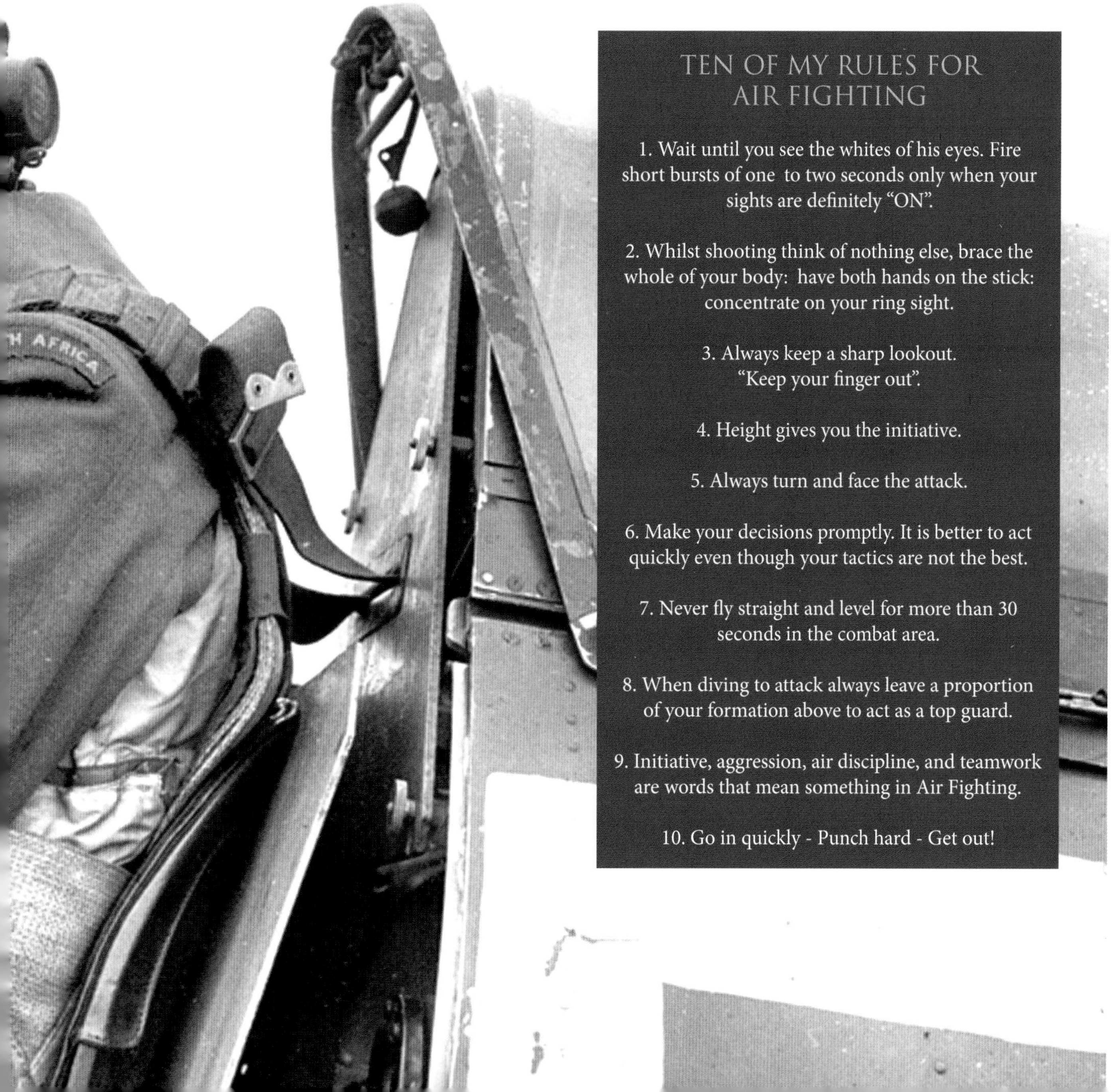

TEN OF MY RULES FOR AIR FIGHTING

1. Wait until you see the whites of his eyes. Fire short bursts of one to two seconds only when your sights are definitely "ON".

2. Whilst shooting think of nothing else, brace the whole of your body: have both hands on the stick: concentrate on your ring sight.

3. Always keep a sharp lookout. "Keep your finger out".

4. Height gives you the initiative.

5. Always turn and face the attack.

6. Make your decisions promptly. It is better to act quickly even though your tactics are not the best.

7. Never fly straight and level for more than 30 seconds in the combat area.

8. When diving to attack always leave a proportion of your formation above to act as a top guard.

9. Initiative, aggression, air discipline, and teamwork are words that mean something in Air Fighting.

10. Go in quickly - Punch hard - Get out!

57

SEPTEMBER 1940 – THE TIDE TURNS

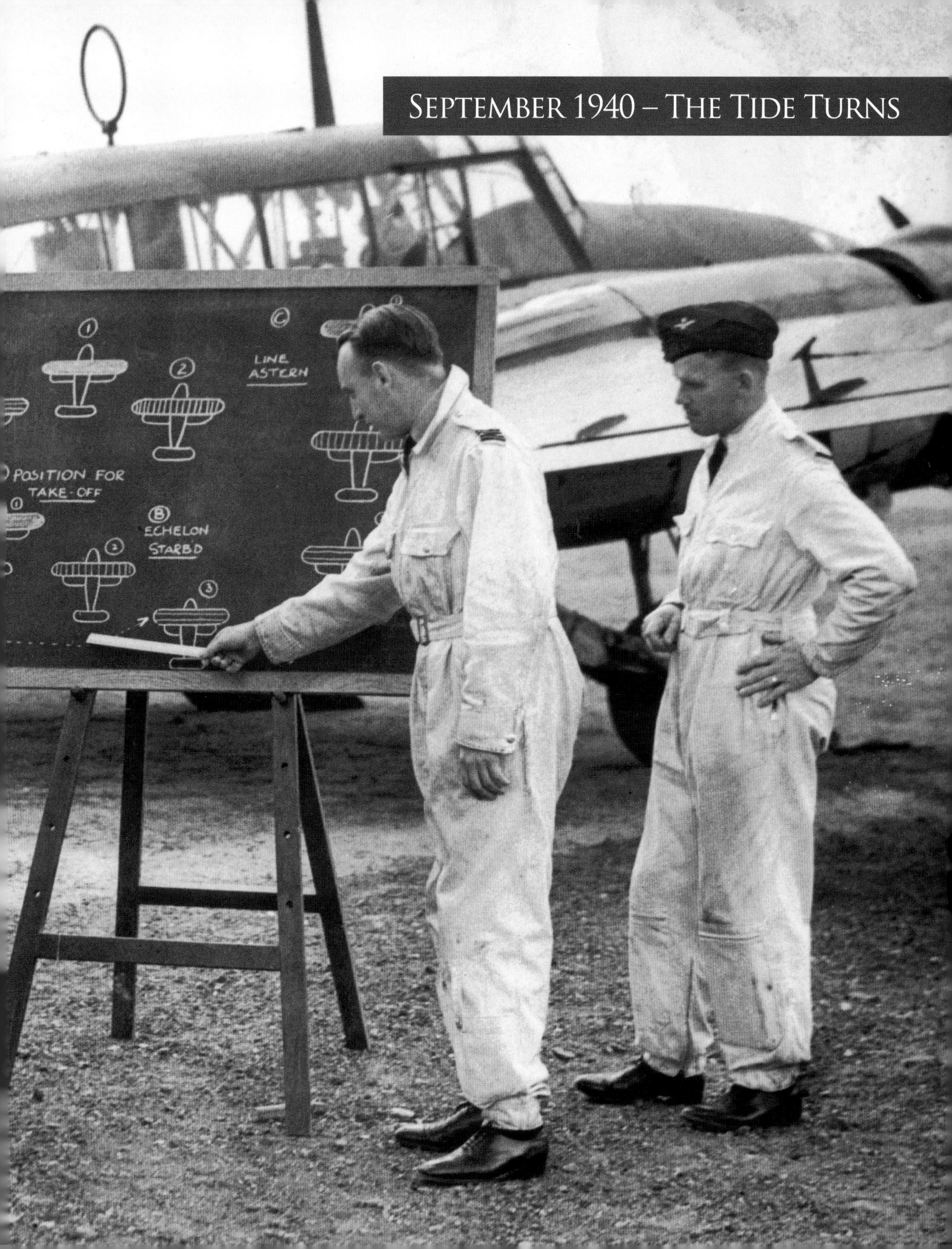

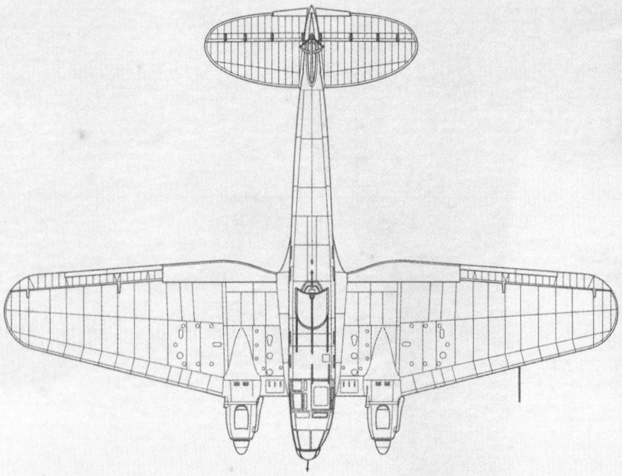

The large-scale air battles and constant pummelling of aerodromes of late August had left the RAF in a parlous state. By 1 September, Dowding was forced to start rearranging his fighting assets. Badly depleted, 151 and 56 Squadrons were withdrawn from the front line and replaced with precious reserves. The airfield at Biggin Hill had been so badly mauled that it could now only accommodate a single squadron instead of its usual four. New pilots - the sprogs - were proving no substitute for the veterans lost. They had a tendency to die quickly and pointlessly, fodder for more experienced adversaries.

The Germans were suffering too. During July and August, they had lost some 800 fighters and bombers and – on the day of Sunday 1 September they had less than 600 frontline serviceable aircraft to put into the air. Behind the scenes, they were desperately struggling to borrow more while repair crews worked flat out to patch what they could. German aircraft production was nowhere near as efficient as British aircraft production under Lord Beaverbrook who was frankly achieving miracles on a daily basis.

That Sunday began with morning raids targeting Eastchurch, Detling, Biggin Hill and London's Docklands. Early afternoon saw a ferocious raid on Lympne aerodrome and a massed raid by 170 Luftwaffe bombers and fighters that managed to punch its way through to Biggin Hill and Kenley airfields. A third wave came in the early evening, bombing Hawkinge and Lympne before inflicting severe damage at Biggin Hill. This time, the operations room was hit and completely destroyed. It was temporarily relocated to a shop in a local village but the airfield was now forced to close and its single remaining squadron – No 79 – relocated to Croydon.

The next morning saw yet another attack on Biggin Hill, as well as raids on the airfields at North Weald, Rochford and Eastchurch. Following the customary morning attacks, a massed German formation

German ground crew writing messages on bombs destined for London

If the Germans had concentrated on the airfields and the radar stations RAF Fighter Command would have had major problems. Biggin Hill was hit on three occasions while I was there and the squadron had to divert to Croydon and West Malling on one occasion. It wasn't good for morale either because when I first went to Biggin Hill I put my private clothing in the sergeant's mess quarters and I never saw them again.

CYRIL BAMBERGER, 610 SQUADRON

We first saw Croydon on the night of 7 September. We flew down from Drem to Abingdon, refuelled and then flew in towards Croydon from that direction. It was about six at night and it was the day, of course, when the Germans got through and bombed the docks so from miles away, before we got to Croydon, we could see the flames and the smoke as the whole of London seemed to be on fire. A huge volume of smoke, black smoke and planes and when we landed at Croydon, just about as it was getting dusk that was our introduction to what it was going to be like. Bunny Currant said 'we're in for trouble now' and there we were but that's what we wanted, what we had come down for.

BOB FOSTER, 605 SQUADRON

of over 250 aircraft swept over Dover shortly after noon. 70 RAF fighters went up to meet them. As was now increasingly common, the Spitfires and Hurricanes were successfully engaged by the Luftwaffe Bf 109s and found it extremely difficult to penetrate through to the bomber formations. As one huge dogfight stretched out at high altitude across the length of Kent, the Luftwaffe bombers ploughed on through to hit Kenley, Hornchurch and Biggin Hill yet once more. Detling and Eastchurch were bombed in early evening raids. At Eastchurch, the bomb dump suffered a direct hit causing a massive fireball that wiped out five fighters on the ground, all the electricity cables, the telephone lines and a number of buildings. Eastchurch was effectively knocked out. It was now declared 'non-operational.' Perhaps worse still, during the day the RAF had lost 25 aircraft to the Luftwaffe's 22. Dowding was now forced to replace both 54 and 85 Squadrons due to their combat losses.

The RAF successfully avoided an early morning trap on 3 September which turned out to be a massive raiding party of Bf 109s pretending to be a bomber formation and looking for combat. Large scale bombing raids followed an hour later against Hornchurch, North Weald and Debden. The raiders' Bf 110 escorts suffered particularly badly in the ensuing dogfights. Seven were accounted for by 310 (Czech) and 19 Squadrons alone.

The afternoon was unnaturally quiet because Goering and his subordinates were planning their next phase of operations at a meeting in the Hague. The day chosen for the German invasion of England was fast approaching and still the RAF had not been comprehensively defeated – despite all their losses and the huge damage inflicted on their airfields. Goering had a new plan to present. The Luftwaffe should turn its attention to London, as ordered by the Fuhrer himself in retaliation for the RAF raids on Berlin. This, surely, would lure the RAF up for a final, decisive showdown.

It took the Luftwaffe another three days to gear up for attacks on London. In the meantime they continued with the strategy of targeting the airfields. Eastchurch and Lympne were hit on the 4th, as well as the radar station at Poling. Low flying Bf 110s, with bombs strung underneath, launched a daring raid on Brooklands and killed almost 90 workers at the Vickers aircraft plant, injuring a further 600. Again, the Bf 110s suffered heavy losses, with five shot down by 253 Squadron on the way in to Brooklands. RAF losses on 4-6 September though were substantial.

Dowding realised he could not cope with such losses for very much longer. In just fourteen days, the RAF had lost 295 fighters. Over

Heinkel He 111 bomber flys over the Isle of Dogs, East End of London

300 pilots had been killed during August and only 260 replacements found for them. Six 11 Group sector stations were on the verge of being knocked out. Dowding now started to think the previously unthinkable. He considered pulling all his remaining fighters out of aerodromes south of London to bases north of the Thames where German bombers couldn't get them. It would leave southern England defenceless – but it would mean that there still would be an operational RAF Fighter Command of a reduced kind when the Germans invaded.

7 September was a beautiful sunny day. After a morning spent touring his airfields, Goering sat down on the cliffs of Cap Gris Nez overlooking the Channel and unpacked a large and lavish picnic. As he tucked in, he was quite convinced that today he would see the end of the RAF. By 4pm, a force of almost 1,000 Luftwaffe fighters and bombers were assembling in the air above – 348 bombers with 617 fighter escorts. It was the greatest flotilla the Luftwaffe had ever put into the air, a formation two miles high and spread across almost 800 square miles

Stunned by the radar signals and reports of *'many hundreds of aircraft'* by the Observer Corps, the RAF initially threw up 11 squadrons and readied all the rest. 10 and 12 Group were put on standby. Unaware that the Luftwaffe were about to change tactics, initially the fighter cover was assigned to protecting the airfields and aircraft factories as on the days before.

It was a complete shock when bombs began falling on the city of London instead. Below, the air raid sirens sounded at about 4.45pm and the Londoners heading for the shelters described the sky as being *'black with aircraft'*. At 5pm, Dorniers and Heinkels released their bombs and incendiaries onto the East End from three miles up. Their initial bomb run was virtually unchallenged except for anti-aircraft fire from the London batteries – but then RAF squadrons began to arrive – 23 of them - diving on both the returning bomber formations and the new ones coming in. Bf 109 escorts slammed into them in turn. Those not in shelters were treated to the sight of what was effectively a thousand aircraft dogfight high above their heads. The Bf 109s had to break off first as their fuel ran low and the bombers were left to fight their way home, harassed by the RAF fighters until their tanks too ran low.

The 'all clear' sounded at 6.15 and civilians emerged from their shelters to find the East End aflame. The bombing had been ferociously accurate. Many docklands warehouses contained combustible produce including the Surrey Docks which held almost 2 million tons of wood supplies. Everything seemed to be on fire and the firemen initially tasked with dealing with the conflagration suffered terrible losses as they were overwhelmed, choked, suffocated and then engulfed in the firestorm. Extinguishing the blaze was impossible – it stretched for nine whole miles along the banks of the Thames. Many small terraced homes had been pummelled in the raid. Whole streets in the East End simply ceased to exist.

British intelligence was now fairly convinced that a German invasion was imminent and the codeword 'Cromwell' was issued, sending all troops to their invasion battlestations. There was chaos as many interpreted the signal wrongly and thought the invasion was already underway. Church bells rang out wildly and reports flooded in of mystery parachutists and fifth columnists on bicycles acting suspiciously.

As night fell over London, German raiders returned in waves that lasted until 5am the following morning, dropping more high explosives and more incendiaries into the fires already raging. 430 people died. 1600 were gravely wounded. It was the first full day of 'the Blitz'. Churchill came out to inspect the damage that morning. He was met with cheers and calls of defiance. When he came upon a shelter that had received a direct hit, he wept openly. That same day, Park saw the devastation for himself as he flew over the stricken city in his personal Hurricane. He was horrified – but he also grasped right there and then that the Germans had made a potentially fatal tactical mistake. By switching their attention to London, they would be giving the RAF airfields a vital breathing space in which to sort themselves out.

The air defence of London had not gone well, however. Only 38 German fighters and bombers had been shot down and in doing so the RAF had lost 28 aircraft of its own. One of the problems had been Park's growing distrust of Leigh-Mallory's 12 Group. At North Weald, Debden and Hornchurch, 11 Group squadrons were told not to take off until the promised air cover from 12 Group actually turned up and so were later and lower into combat. Leigh-Mallory's much vaunted Big Wing had also seen combat, with 36 fighters of 242, 302 and 19 Squadrons flying under Douglas Bader – but to little effect. RAF morale, already at a low ebb from weeks of exhausting fighting, dropped still lower at the sight of the forces the Luftwaffe had put into the air, while the Luftwaffe pilots were greatly encouraged by a very successful first daylight raid against the capital. *'London is in flames!'* proclaimed Goering.

The bombers returned at 7.30pm on the 8th. As they came in from the east following the Thames, the pilots tuned their cockpit radios into the BBC and listened to dance music as they bombed. Below, the public were already suspicious of the adequacy of official bomb shelters and started to pack into the Underground stations instead. At first the authorities tried to stop them but quickly relented under sheer weight of numbers. Two hundred bombers raided London that night, killing

Pilots from 19 Squadron 'scramble' for the cameras at Fowlmere, a satellite airfield of Duxford, in September 1940

Hurricanes of 501 Squadron take off from Gravesend, after being refuelled and rearmed

another 400 Londoners, knocking out the railways south of the Thames and setting 12 more major fires.

On Monday 9th, 605 and 607 squadrons managed to disrupt and break up a raid by Do 17s and He 111s heading for London. 19, 242 and 310 squadrons of 12 Group joined in the defence of London, deciding themselves to get involved rather than stick to their assigned role of airfield defence and a large German force was met with unexpected strength over South London. Faced with determined resistance by 253 Squadron Hurricanes and 303 (Polish), many bombers just dropped their loads early and fled for home. They were expecting a clear run. The RAF was quickly re-gearing to meet the threat to London. Most of the day's raids were driven off and 28 Luftwaffe aircraft downed at a cost of 21 RAF fighters. From his HQ, Leigh-Mallory shot off a snotty memo complaining that an 11 Group fighter had shot down a German aircraft inside 12 Group's *'turf'*. *'Full explanation required,'* he ended – and he meant it. Park must have been incandescent, especially as Leigh-Mallory's pilots had yet again ignored his explicit orders to defend his airfields.

By night, the Luftwaffe came again. Under cover of darkness, it was almost impossible to find let alone stop the bomber fleets. Another 370 Londoners were killed in the night raids as Madame Tussaud's, the Natural History Museum and the Royal Courts of Justice all burned. The 10th was a similar story. Two more large scale daylight raids were launched against London on 11 September. German losses amounted to around 25 aircraft but the RAF lost 29 fighters in intercepting the raids. That night 200 Luftwaffe aircraft returned to pound London once more, while others struck Liverpool. Out in the North Sea, German mine laying aircraft worked tirelessly under cover of darkness to pen the Royal Navy in, in preparation for the invasion. As the Luftwaffe flew in, so RAF Bomber and Coastal Command flew out to bomb the German invasion barges along the French and Belgian coasts. At least a hundred barges were sunk in the raids, but the RAF lost 15 aircraft to German fighters and thick anti-aircraft fire. Bomber Command returned the following night and reported destroying another 70 invasion barges as well as hitting German troop camps around the barge ports and inflicting heavy casualties. Two British bombers were shot down by anti-aircraft fire.

The late morning of Friday 13th saw a succession of lone raiders turning up over London at less than ten minute intervals to unload their bomb loads. Central London was hit, from Parliament Square to Buckingham Palace. By night the attacks on the capital were much heavier with waves of bombers coming in at irregular intervals almost until dawn. The capital's anti-aircraft guns got one bomber and a Blenheim night fighter accounted for another.

Saturday 14th saw early morning raids by Ju 88s against a number of radar stations, while Heinkels and Dorniers bombed Brighton and Eastbourne. South London was attacked again in the afternoon, and ominously, RAF interceptors came off significantly worst in engagements with the bomber escorts. Over the day, the Luftwaffe had succeeded in shooting down 13 fighters – and a Spitfire had accidentally shot down a Hurricane from 73 Squadron. The Germans had lost a total of just seven aircraft.

Spitfires of 65 Squadron fly in perfect formation

Londoners take shelter in the subway tunnels

The days of 11-14 September gave the RAF a vital breathing space. They might have been just four days, but now Dowding and Park had time to find vital replacements while their pilots rested and recuperated. Mechanics repaired much-needed fighters. Ground crews filled bomb craters on the airfields. New recruits even managed some training. Goering however was told that the RAF was on the verge of collapse. It was disorganised and increasingly ineffectual. The fighting force, he believed, was down to its very last 50 Spitfires. He decided to test those reports…

The weather was perfect on the morning of Sunday 15 September. Park knew this meant the Germans would be coming in force. By coincidence, Winston Churchill was visiting his Uxbridge HQ that day, along with his wife. They would be there to witness the epic battle that was to follow.

At around 10.45am, radar reports started coming in of a massive German force assembling over the Pas de Calais – a force two miles wide and nine thousand feet thick in the air. It comprised a hundred Dorniers escorted by two hundred Bf 109 escorts. Park had no doubt the target was to be London, All 11 Group squadrons were readied in a matter of minutes and 10 and 12 Group notified of the need to help. Park had devised a new tactic. He knew he had no hope of stopping the force getting through but – if his fighters could just keep the escorts busy and entangled over southern England, they would use up their fuel quicker and would have to turn for home earlier. That meant the bombers would be unescorted – and more vulnerable – for longer.

Spitfires of 72 and 92 Squadrons hit the Luftwaffe formation over Maidstone. The Bf 109s went after them, only to be bounced by 603 Squadron. More Bf 109s got sucked in to aid their fellow Messerschmitts, creating a hole through which 253 and 501 Squadrons managed to get at the Dorniers. More and more RAF squadrons piled into the epic aerial battle as the formation progressed over Kent, until the Germans found themselves under attack by 250 fighters from 23 different squadrons. A further six squadrons joined the fight as the bomber fleet reached the suburbs of south London, then five squadrons of the Duxford Wing of 12 Group came diving down on the Dorniers just as they were dropping their bombs. The bomber formations shattered, individual planes wheeling and accelerating everywhere in a desperate attempt to escape. Having broken formation there was little their escorts could do to protect them. RAF fighters harassed them all the way south back over the Channel as well as up the length of the Thames into the North Sea.

As the RAF squadrons raced home to land, refuel and rearm, reports came in of another colossal German aerial armada sweeping in in three waves – a total of 150 bombers escorted this time by 400 fighters. They crossed the coast near Dungeness at 2.15pm, spread across ten full miles of sky. Spitfires from 41 and 603 Squadrons hit them over Romney Marshes and managed to shoot down two of the Dorniers before the Messerschmitt escorts fell on them. 73 Squadron were next, destroying three bombers off Maidstone. Spitfires from 66 and 72 Squadrons intercepted them over Dartford, quickly reinforced by four more squadrons. Hurricanes of 303 (Polish) hit bombers and their Bf 110 fighters over Gravesend. 213 and 607 Squadron Hurricanes out of Tangmere punched into the bombers above the borders of Surrey,

On off duty time we were able to get into the West End being a half hour tube ride from Hornchurch and during those nights we did go into London we were at the receiving end of the bombing, could hear that going on, the anti aircraft going and in the mornings when we came home or even when we got into London after stand down it was those people who were taking refuge in the tube stations who were all there with their bedding and places lined up ready to spend a night in the underground shelters of the underground tube stations. It was the same in the morning going back to go on duty. You could see the terrible life that a lot of the civilians had to cope with. If they'd been either chosen to go into the shelters or forced into the shelters by lack of housing of their own or their own houses having been damaged, we were very close to what civilians were having to put up with.

KEITH LAWRENCE, 234 SQUADRON

shooting down several in their initial attack. Wherever the bombers flew, they flew into more trouble.

The nerve of the Luftwaffe bomber pilots began to crack under the sheer weight of the assaults on them. The formations teetered. Some individual bombers broke formation and fled. Others dumped their bombs. Those who held their nerve faced a wall of flak from London's recently improved AA defences as they reached the outskirts of the city. After negotiating that they suddenly found themselves facing 15 more squadrons of RAF fighters, comprising a Big Wing of five 12 Group Squadrons and ten 11 Group squadrons. It was a truly terrifying sight. The German bomber formations - suddenly faced with a sky full of fresh hostile fighters lost what was left of their discipline and their formations began to come apart. They dropped their bombs pretty much just anywhere and then tried to flee for home. They were harassed by fighters every single step of the way.

Over in France, the sight of one damaged bomber after another limping its way home and then spilling out wounded and dying air crew told its own story. The RAF were far from finished and something pretty much decisive had just happened. Back across the Channel the RAF pilots and their commanders knew that they had achieved something pretty incredible. There were reports of 183 German aircraft shot down. It wasn't true – the real number was fifty six – but it felt to the fighter pilots as if they had decimated the Luftwaffe that day. RAF losses stood at just 26 – and a full half of the pilots shot down had survived.

The next day, bad weather closed in and there was little activity. Goering refused to believe anything significant had happened but rapidly changed his tactics all the same. There would be no more large scale bomber fleets, just small groups escorted by massed fighter formations. They would continue to bomb London, but they would also go back to attacking RAF airfields and aircraft factories too. He could not resist yet another jibe at his fighter pilots for not doing better to protect the bombers. That night, the Luftwaffe pounded the capital to show it was not defeated, using 170 bombers.

By daybreak on 17 September German fighters tried to entice their RAF counterparts out for dogfights with varying degrees of success. By night 268 bombers hit London while RAF bombers struck against German shipping and blew up a massive arms dump intended for use in the invasion at Dunkirk. On the 18th the Germans tried the same tactic to lure out the fighters with less success but also launched a daylight bombing raid against London comprising Ju 88 bombers. It was hit hard over Gravesend and then again over the Thames Estuary. At the end of the day the Luftwaffe had lost a further 15 aircraft compared with 12 RAF fighters. By night, Bomber Command hit the invasion ports and the troop camps once more with some 200 aircraft. In response Hitler ordered the barges to be widely dispersed to avoid more losses, as well as troop concentrations to be broken up and moved inland for greater protection. The invasion was effectively on hold.

The German High Command still held vague hopes of destroying the RAF and continued with its tactic of sending over formations of Bf 109s to fight a war of attrition against their RAF counterparts. The RAF continued to avoid contact and so minimise casualties wherever possible. Night raids on London also continued. RAF Blenheim and Defiant night fighters sent up against the night bombers proved largely ineffectual. On the 24 and 25th, Luftwaffe raids concentrated on aircraft factories, first the Spitfire works at Woolston near Southampton and then Filton near Bristol. 100 workers died when a shelter was hit at the Spitfire works during a fast raid by Bf 109s carrying bombs and over 250 workers died in a Heinkel raid on Filton. The Spitfire works were hit again on the 26th, killing another 30 people and the factory had to stop production. Thankfully, it was by now not the only site producing Spitfires. Filton was targeted for attack again on the 27th, but the raiding He 111s were intercepted before they could reach the plant. They dropped their bombs prematurely and then fled for the protection of their Bf 110 escorts who were waiting for them over Swanage.

The 27th also saw a return to daylight formation bombing raids against London. This time, the Luftwaffe tried the unusual combination of Bf 110s carrying bombs with a Bf 109 escort. They were driven off, as was a later force of 55 Ju 88s and a final noon assault by 300 German aircraft. In all the fighting, the Luftwaffe lost 54 aircraft to the RAF's 28. Further, smaller Luftwaffe raids were beaten off on Saturday 28th but the RAF suffered grievously as the BF 109 escorts used their height advantage to the full. 16 RAF fighters were lost while the Luftwaffe lost just 3 aircraft.

Little happened on 29 September due to increasingly bad weather but conditions improved on the 30th and the Germans came again. By 9am, twelve squadrons were in action against two formations of German aircraft, each 100 strong. Faced with determined RAF opposition, most of the bombers gave up while still over Maidstone, dumping their loads and fleeing for home. A later formation of 100 bombers and 200 fighters proved to be made of sterner stuff, but was still extensively disrupted. Some bombers got through to London, but they were badly mauled on both the approach and return. The Luftwaffe lost 50 aircraft during the day, compared with RAF losses of 20. 12 of the RAF pilots survived and the majority would be back with their squadrons within 24 hours.

The number 88 bus lies in a large crater in the road in Balham, London, the morning after a German air raid

DOGFIGHTING

Was dogfighting an art? Or controlled chaos? Or maybe just luck? Well these seven pilots who were in the thick of the fighting all had their own views of what happened in a dogfight

Once you picked out your target you separated, your sections would separate from each other and then the aircraft within your section separated and picked out their target. If you had been vectored onto the bombers particularly you go in and shoot until you have to pull away because you overtake, you've got overtaking speed, and you get in as much firing at the target as you can and after that you pull up hoping to find some of your fellow squadron pilots but as like as not you will be left alone with the sight of a few enemy aircraft and it's then that you've got to start to weave, not to fly straight and level but to be on the alert and take the complete look out, looking for any remaining targets there might be and fighters that might still be hunting for whatever Hurricanes and Spitfires they could find and this is where we learned very fast how one needed to fly to disengage and return to base from an empty sky. As often as not you'd return by yourself as did all the others in ones or in pairs as we'd been split up by either dogfights or having gone through the bombers we'd been broken up by individual engagements and then had to find your own way home. The squadron would take perhaps 20 minutes to arrive back and after 20 minutes those of us that were gathered together in the dispersal hut began to wonder why so and so wasn't back, or so and so still hasn't phoned. As often as not he'd baled out or had been shot down and force landed somewhere. The odd time he'd bought it but that's the way it was . The squadron would be gathered together, the spare aircraft would be put into the line and we'd go back on readiness ready for the next scramble, the aircraft having been rearmed and refuelled.

KEITH LAWRENCE

For a few seconds you're focusing on the aircraft in front of you but not for much longer than that. After all, whatever you do, it's not quite like the First World War where you were dicing around, looping the loop and all this sort of thing. The whole thing is over and done with in seconds. You go in, you attack, you either hit or you don't and you break away. And then you're conscious that someone may be after you. It's difficult to describe. The adrenalin's flowing and you're trying to do two things at once. You're trying to shoot down something else but on the other hand you're conscious that someone else may be after you. And I think obviously with a lot of chaps who were shot down the second thing happened. You forgot about the chap behind you.

BOB FOSTER

It's really up to your controller, your ground controller, who is watching your squadron and where it is in relation to the raid he is vectoring you on to. First of all, if it's possible and he can give you height, he could give you enough height to gain, to be above the German fighters or the bombers he can vector you down onto them and put you up sun first of all but it depended on the fighter controller and they varied greatly in skills to manoeuvre their squadrons into the right positions, hardly ever for a head on attack because the closing speeds of the two aircraft would be something like 700mph I suppose and the length of burst a fighter could get in at a closing speed of 700mph was pretty well ineffectual unless he happened to hit the pilot head on. So the normal was for the fighter controller to bring the squadron abeam of the formation.

KEITH LAWRENCE

Well it all happens very quickly. You suddenly break cloud, look around and you realise somebody's above you diving down at you so you have to break. You try and keep with your leader or your number two but it all happens very, very quickly. There's not much time to think. It's an explosive situation. When you're more in control and you're as a full squadron and you see a formation below you and you're attacking, that's much more simple and organised. I remember flying with the first cannon-armed Hurricane. It was flown by Flight Lieutenant Smith who was the 'B' Flight commander. He had two cannons under the wing and that was the first trial. I was flying his number two that day and I was absolutely fascinated and I stuck with him when he attacked these bombers, these Heinkels, and he blew bloody great holes and we were delighted to think we were at last getting a bigger gun. We realised that our .303 machine gun wasn't big enough but when you had the organisation and you were attacking as a formation that was fine. The more difficult one to cope with was when you were bounced and you just broke. Sometimes you broke and you looked around and there was nobody else in sight so the thing to do was to get back to base and rearm, refuel and be ready to rejoin your mates when they came back.

JOHN ELLACOMBE

Its almost impossible to describe. Its just a mass of aeroplanes coming and going in all directions, very close to you, you can hear their engines

and then you try and chase somebody. The thrill of having a good burst at him and knowing you've hit him. You haven't got time to claim him because you break away because there's somebody about to have a go at you. And this is coming back to what I said at the beginning. Never stay still for more than 20 seconds. Don't get carried away if you think you've got somebody. If you tickle him up a bit at least you've put him off but if you follow him down nine times out of ten he would have a number two and they'd have a go at you so it was just total confusion. Warm work. I remember thinking clearly one day 'What am I doing in this lot? This is bloody dangerous' but its a very difficult question to answer because you react differently in every combat really but if it's a general mix-up. You were far too busy shooting and avoiding being shot at.

Geoffrey Wellum

Well the doctrine, the only doctrine we had was to get as close to the aeroplane as possible, to shoot and to make certain that we weren't being looked at ourselves so that was the only doctrine. Make absolutely certain that you had your eyes wide open everywhere, behind you and in front of you and to get as close in as possible. We had to get close in with the machine guns in the wings, we had to get in to about 250 feet which is very close and fairly bumpy as you have the slipstream but that was the only doctrine, get in close and fire as little as possible but as effectively as possible.

Billy Drake

Well Hogan (Squadron Leader Harry Hogan) used to bring the squadron up to head on attacks. It was always going in from the front. In the distance you'd see a big black cloud, looked like a thunderstorm, but it actually was a formation of probably 200 German bombers coming in. Above them you could see the 109s as they were turning and twisting above the bombers to protect them and he would take us in on these head on attacks where we hoped we could get there before the 109s could come down on to us to protect their bombers and invariably we would because we'd go in on a head on attack. You'd go straight through the bombers. You'd fire your guns. If there was any knocked down, of course the senior blokes would claim them and down you'd go and that was it. You'd then be attacked by these 109s and it was a matter of looking after yourself then. It was every man for himself then and eventually, after a few minutes, Hogan would call up and say 'Reform' using coded words of course, reform over Ashford or somewhere and telling us to reform at a certain height and we'd go back as a squadron again and then he'd call us together and we'd go in for another attack, that's what used to happen.

Tony Pickering

Dogfighting was chaos for a matter of almost a minute or two minutes. Occasionally you chased something, fighters against fighters, you might chase something which may be for five or ten minutes but the actual dogfight itself, something flashed across your gunsight, you fired your guns and hoped you'd hit. Quite often you missed them altogether but there was no First World War type of dogfights. They may have occurred on odd occasions but I never experienced anything like that.

Cyril Bamberger

Colour image taken during the filming of 1969 movie Battle of Britain

Foreign Pilots

It's sometimes overlooked, but it is a fact that a good 20% of all the fighter pilots who flew with the RAF during the Battle of Britain were not British. It's estimated that 574 pilots who fought were 'foreign' - and they made perhaps a decisive contribution to the final outcome of the Battle.

Naturally, one of the biggest single contributions came from the Commonwealth. Over 30 Australians served with Fighter Command during the battle, the most celebrated of whom was Flight Lieutenant Paterson 'Pat' Hughes, of 234 Squadron flying Spitfires. Hughes scored a total of 14 kills, starting with a Ju 88 as early as 8 July. He died a victim of his own love of 'getting in close', when he accidentally collided with a Do 17 bomber on 7 September. 83 Canadian pilots fought in the Battle, Some served with individual RAF Squadrons and 26 flew Hurricanes with 1 Squadron RCAF (Later 401 Squadron). 135 New Zealanders fought in the Battle, with the highest scoring pilot being Flight Lieutenant Colin Gray, who shot down 14 enemy aircraft during the Battle while flying Spitfires with 54 Squadron. He was a sheep musterer by trade who had originally been refused a place in the RAF on medical grounds. South Africa contributed 25 pilots, including the legendary 'Sailor' Malan and Pilot Officer Albert 'Zulu' Lewis, who shot down three Bf 109s in a single action during the Battle of France and who had scored 18 confirmed 'kills' before he was finally shot down and incapacitated by burns on 28 September. Of the four Rhodesian pilots who took part, two were killed in action.

30 Belgians took part, spread across regular RAF squadrons, but the largest contingent served with 609 Squadron. Surprisingly, less than fifteen French pilots flew and fought. No one is quite sure how many Americans took part in the Battle. Because they were liable to face criminal prosecution for breaking strict American neutrality, some undoubtedly signed up claiming to be Canadian and were accepted with no questions asked. The best guess is that there were 11 or 12 American citizens flying and fighting with the RAF during the Battle. They included ex-barnstormers, an Olympic bobsled champion nicknamed 'The King of Speed' and Vernon Keough, who was only 4'10" tall and who consequently had to scramble with a plump cushion under each arm so he could sit on them and see over the instrument panel in his cockpit. They called him 'Shorty'. The 'King of Speed' Billy Fiske crash-landed his Hurricane at Tangmere on 16 August. He was taken to the hospital with burns to the face and hands and died the next day from shock.

The Republic of Ireland was also strictly neutral, but that didn't stop ten Irish citizens from volunteering to take part. The most famous Irish fighter pilot was undoubtedly Brendan 'Paddy' Finucane, an exceptionally young and good looking Dubliner who became – quite literally – a pin up boy for the RAF during the Battle and who received volumes of fan mail from smitten girls (one even wrote to say how much she wished she could nurse him after Finucane was shot down). He scored two 'kills' and two probables flying his Shamrock-decorated Spitfire with 65 Squadron during the Battle of Britain but went on to run up a tally which may be as high as 32. Surviving the Battle he went on to become the RAF's youngest ever wing commander in January 1942. On 15 July that year, his Spitfire was hit by ground fire over France and he was too low to bail out. As he plunged into the Channel his last words were, 'this is it, chaps'. He was 21 years old.

The largest contingent of 'foreign' pilots who took part in the Battle were Eastern European, essentially Czechs or Poles. They had escaped their doomed nations, somehow made it to France to fight the Nazis during the Blitzkrieg and – when France fell – crossed the Channel to fight on. Once here, they fell victim to a number of prejudices and concerns that the RAF High Command held about them. Both Czechoslovakia and Poland had fallen easily to the Nazis, which reflected badly on their air forces. Few of them spoke any English, which gave the RAF grave concerns about their ability to follow orders. They were wild and reckless in the air. They were rebellious and ill-disciplined and 'a rough bunch of chaps' on the ground. They reputedly liked a drink or two. After being held under armed guard in Blackpool for some weeks, they were largely corralled into two Polish and one Czech Squadron.

Consequently, both the Poles and the Czechs were put into training (both flying and language) and missed the first month or more of the Battle of Britain. When pilot casualties drove the RAF to think the nearly unthinkable, they were finally allowed to fly. It was more like they had been unleashed - and their combat abilities staggered the previously dubious RAF. What they did not appreciate was that the Czechs and the Poles had in fact received expert flying instruction with their native air forces – but they had been given very poor aircraft in the past. They were also – by RAF standards – very combat experienced, fighting at home, then in France. They had an excellent understanding of dogfighting tactics – and they knew what they were doing. They were older than average – 24 compared to the average age of a British fighter pilot which was 20. And most of all they were motivated. Many possessed a seething hatred of the Nazis, having had their homelands conquered and pillaged, and wanted nothing but bloody revenge. 147 Poles and 87 Czechs flew and fought in the Battle. Polish pilots claimed 203 enemy aircraft during the Battle, and 29 of them died. Dowding later wrote of the Poles:

'Had it not been for the magnificent material contributed by the Polish squadrons and their unsurpassed gallantry, I hesitate to say that the outcome of the Battle would have been the same.'

Four Czech-Slovak pilots from a Hurricane Fighter Squadron, watching some of their colleagues in flight

When I came to in the other bed was Frank Czajkowsky, our Polish pilot. He had a bullet in his shoulder and in his legs. He used to get in a wheelchair and disappear and go round the hospital and he came back one day and he said 'There's a ward out there and it's full of Germans and there's one in there you shot down on 24 August, one of the Heinkel bomber crew' and he said 'They're very interesting men to talk to'. He spoke absolutely fluent German. The next day one of the young doctors came in and said 'Ellacombe, stop that bugger going into that ward. He's telling them we're going to get them better, interrogate them and then shoot them and they're not getting much better' so Frank was not allowed to go back into that ward.

JOHN ELLACOMBE, 151 SQUADRON

303 Squadron (Polish)

Flying Hurricanes out of Northolt, 303 (Polish) Squadron soon earned a proud reputation as one of the elite RAF Squadrons during the Battle of Britain.

However, 303 Squadron was very late to enter the battle, due to doubts about them by RAF commanders. And so they trained and trained. They saw the other two Squadrons stationed at Northolt – one British and one Canadian – flying and fighting every day while they continued 'training'. They were told that they could not fly until they could speak English and were given strange training exercises like cycling in strict formation around Ruislip with radio transmitters attached to their bikes, practicing following orders.

They became ever more ill-disciplined and truculent. They wanted nothing more than to kill Nazis but – if they were prohibited from doing that – they would do the next best thing and mix it up with the hated Irish Guard soldiers who were posted to secure their air base. After one mass punch up at a dance hall in Ruislip, a number of Irish Guards were hospitalised. After another altercation, the Poles and the Irish actually started shooting at one another and the fighting only stopped when both sides ran out of ammunition. The incident was hushed up.

They were led by a short, English ex-stockbroker called Squadron Leader Ronald 'Boozy' Kellett who delighted his Polish comrades with his eccentric ways and his love of driving everywhere in his own Rolls Royce. His nickname might also offer another reason for which he was respected. A genuinely strange man, in his way as undisciplined as his Polish charges, he was known to try and train pilots by pointing to a Hurricane and then flapping his arms furiously and yelling 'fly!'

The squadron scored its first 'kill' before even becoming operational. On 30 August, whilst on a training flight, Flight officer Ludwik Paszkiewicz spotted a Bf 110. He asked permission to engage and when he got no reply, just went ahead and did it anyway, closing to point blank range before blasting it from the skies. On his return to Northolt, Paszkiewicz was given a public roasting in front of his comrades by Kellett, but then heartily congratulated in private by him. Kellett then rang his superiors and requested 303 Squadron become officially operational. They were given operational status from the very next day – and scored 4 confirmed 'kills' and two further probables.

303 Squadron quickly proved their proficiency in air combat. On 5 September, they shot down three Heinkel 111s and five of their Bf 109 fighter escorts for the loss of just one aircraft. On 11 September 303 Squadron shot down three Do 17 and four He 111 bombers, as well as two Bf 110s and a BF 109 for the loss of two aircraft. They were also in the thick of the fight on the crucial day of 15 September. Mid-morning, the Poles shot down two Do 17s, a Bf 110 and six Bf 109 escorts over London - and returned in the afternoon to claim another four kills.

When it was discovered that the Poles were more effective than regular RAF squadrons, the censors worked hard to cover up the fact – but

Pilots of 303 Polish Fighter Squadron RAF after returning from a fighter sortie

word still got out. One newspaper called them 'the glamour boys of England'. Praise flooded in for the Polish contribution to the battle, even from Downing Street. Squadron Leader Kellett replied to Churchill's warm words to the effect that talk was fine but they'd rather have a crate of whiskey thank you very much. They got it. A local school in Ruislip had a collection for the airmen and all clubbed in to buy them 450 cigarettes. Another school in Glasgow proudly sent them a postal order for ten shillings. On 26 September King George VI came to pay a personal visit. While he was there, there was a squadron scramble and the King was almost knocked off his feet as the Poles lost any interest in His Majesty and ran for their fighters. Skilful and lethally aggressive, the pilots of 303 Squadron went on to claim a total of 126 kills during the Battle of Britain – the highest score of any of the 66 Squadrons which participated – even though they had not become operational until the dying days of August 1940. They also set the record for the highest number of kills in a single month (more than double that of the nearest squadron) and for the most kills for the fewest losses. Their desire to kill Germans at any price is amply illustrated by the actions of Sergeant Stanislaw Karubin who, whilst chasing a Bf 109 at treetop height on 2 September, suddenly found his guns had run dry. Undeterred, he flew directly over the top of the Bf 109, matched it for speed and then gradually dropped his height, forcing the German pilot right into the ground.

The End of the Invasion Threat

On 17 September, Hitler finally lost faith in any and all invasion plans. The events of 15 September in the air over Britain had convinced him that the RAF were far from defeated. He ordered Seelowe to be postponed indefinitely – and the invasion barges and waiting troops to be scattered so as to prevent yet more attrition caused by Bomber Command raids. It was a frank acknowledgement that Goering had failed to destroy the RAF and that bombing the capital would not lead to British pleas for surrender. On October 12 Hitler agreed to delay Seelowe until 1941. It was never effective again.

Pilot and co-pilot of a Whitley bomber before setting off on a raid

October 1940 – Messerschmitt Month

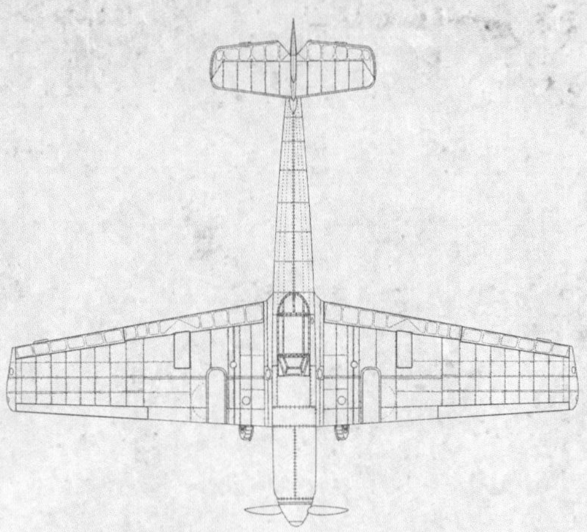

With the invasion plan for England now on hold and the RAF increasingly successful at intercepting and disrupting bomber formations during the daylight hours the Luftwaffe finally took the decision to end the practice of regular large scale bomber raids over England in daylight.

A few small-scale or solo daylight bomber raids did continue, the bulk of which were carried out by Ju 88s in the Luftwaffe fleet which were less vulnerable because of their speed. A solo Ju 88 raid on 3 October succeeded in breaching defences and bombing the de Havilland aircraft works at Hatfield. The aircraft was later shot down by AA guns. The next day, another marauding Ju 88 was blown apart in mid-air over Southwold in Suffolk by the guns of Squadron Leader Bob Tuck, the commanding officer of 257 Squadron. On 7 October, 25 Ju 88s with 50 Bf 110 escorts hit the Westland aircraft factory at Yeovil in Somerset. Two Ju 88s were downed as well as seven of their escorts, which were hit hard by the Hurricanes of 601 Squadron. It was only the late intervention of a nearby Bf 109 formation that stopped the losses being higher still.

The Luftwaffe were also still infuriated by the RAF largely ignoring the fighter formations trying to provoke dogfights and so came up with an ingenious new tactic. A third of the Bf 109 fleet were now converted to carry 250kg bombs which made them far more difficult to ignore. Unless they were stopped, Messerschmitts could now attack strategic targets. On days with good flying conditions, up to one hundred largely solo fighter-bombers – now designated Bf 109E-7 'Jabos' - would range inland as far as London. They hit airfield after airfield, raided Portsmouth and Southampton docks and almost succeeded in knocking out all train services after blitzing Waterloo Station. It was only the limitation to the bombloads these small fighters could carry

Pilots of JG 53, nicknamed 'Pik-As', or Ace of Spades, one of the Luftwaffe's most successful fighter wings shooting down 112 RAF aircraft in 200 operations during the battle

that stopped them from being a more effective threat.

The pilots of these 'Jabo' flights, however, were told by Goering that they were a form of punishment: Fighters were now being turned into bombers because they had failed to adequately protect the bombers. It was hardly conducive to good morale and some Bf 109 pilots deliberately dumped their bombloads at random to show their contempt. (Eventually even Goering got the message that he had gone too far and tried to bribe himself back into his pilots' good books by offering them all a free skiing holiday in the new year).

In late October observers and interceptor pilots alike were surprised to see the unfamiliar profiles of Italian warplanes in the air over England, as Mussolini's Regia Aeronautica raced to get some battle honours in the closing days of the Battle of Britain. Mussolini despatched 200 aircraft to join the campaign, operating out of airfields in Belgium captured by the Germans during the Blitzkrieg. They were not, on the whole, warmly welcomed by their German allies. On 25 October, a flight of Fiat Br 20s bombed Harwich and the Italians would continue to take part in occasional raids until 7 February 1941. During that time, they lost 24 aircraft and failed to succeed in shooting down even a single RAF aircraft.

29 October saw the Luftwaffe fly one last significant daylight bombing raid by their bombing fleet. They were joined again that day by a number of bombers from the Italian Air Force. The Italians attacked Ramsgate while the Luftwaffe went for Portsmouth and London. Most of the raiders were disrupted and chased off by efficient RAF interception. The Italians fled when met with determined anti-aircraft fire. Over 20 axis aircraft were lost during the raid. The same day, 100 bomb-carrying 'Jabos' were successfully intercepted and eight of them shot down in less than ten minutes. The others just dropped their bombs and turned for home. The RAF had found the measure of the Messerschmitt threat. It confirmed what Goering and his commanders already knew.

The end of October merely confirmed that the RAF were in charge now. The month had seen 379 Luftwaffe aircraft shot down for the loss of 185 RAF fighters.

Today - 31 October is officially regarded as the last day of the Battle of Britain. It was quiet due to rain on that day, and there were no losses. However it would be a mistake to think that all aerial battles ceased upon that date. The very next day, 1 November, saw Ju 87s with a fighter escort tangling with fighters from 74 and 92 Squadrons out of Biggin Hill. In a separate action, fighter ace Squadron Leader Archibald McKellar of 605 Squadron was shot down and killed while intercepting a flight of 'Jabos' over Kent. On 7 October he had shot down five Bf109s in a single day.

The Battle of Britain might be over, but the Blitz would continue with full ferocity. From the end of October, the Luftwaffe concentrated on its night raids, and the bombing of London would continue almost every single night until May 1941 when the bombers were called away to prepare for the invasion of Russia. Most nights would see an average of 150 aircraft over the capital. On nights with a full moon, that number might increase to 300 bombers. Over 20,000 people would die in London and around the same number in other towns and cities around the British Isles. The raids were little more than spite now, albeit on a grand scale. Hitler had largely lost interest in Britain and was looking east to those he regarded as his true enemies – the Soviets.

Firemen at work in a bomb damaged street in London

A British soldier guarding a German Messerschmitt Me109, which was intercepted over the English Channel and shot down by a Spitfire patrol.

Night fighting in the battle

After a very busy Dunkirk operation 92 Squadron was withdrawn from the front line to Pembrey in South Wales to rest and bring in new pilots. Allan Wright had a number of confirmed and unconfirmed kills during the frantic ten days of the Dunkirk operation but perhaps his most unexpected victory came on 29 August while patrolling Bristol at night.

It was very much a cat and mouse affair, not what the rest of the battle was like at all. Anyway, we were sent to a field, two fields locked together, a flarepath was made up of six rows of bulbs and you couldn't see it until you'd found it. We used to have a coloured light and they'd put it five miles from the airfield and you had to remember where the airfield was in relation to it when you got back and then find the flarepath and get down so that was tricky for a start. Then we had no homing device at all in the aeroplane so first of all they had to pick you up when you took off and the way they did that was to tell you to fly left or right and see which blip on their screen was the one that did that. Sometimes they got it right and sometimes they didn't so sometimes you were up there wondering when you would be under control or even whether you would get back to base or not. On one particular occasion I was sent up and I patrolled, I think they had lights on the ground you could patrol, if you were told to so you'd do that while they decided if they wanted to control you and I wanted to ask questions so called up and didn't get an answer. I did this several times and then I realised that somebody had left his transmitter on down there and I heard them talking to each other and asking for cups of tea etc while I was sitting out there in the black depending on them for my life apart from anything else. Anyhow on this occasion I was told to go after a bogey which was near Bristol at 20,000 feet so I flew in that direction and saw the searchlights obviously looking for something and as I got nearer to it there was this one in the searchlight. As soon as I got up to it the searchlights came back to me and the ack ack came on me instead of them, this was again something that occurred because it was easier to follow something directly than try and get ahead of it so I did what I had to do which was to flash a light I had underneath which tells them to stop firing. So they stopped firing and the lights went out as well so it was black except for the stars up there, lots of stars, black night and I was looking around wondering 'Where is the bugger?' and flying in the sort of direction I thought it was and I saw a red glow and another red glow next to it and I thought that must be it so I went after these two glows. It was difficult to concentrate the speeds and not look in the cockpit at all but eventually I did get into position and I went on firing at this thing and eventually flames came from one of them and that made it easier. I kept going on one then the other and then they both went out as it curled away and then I couldn't find it anymore so I came back but in fact both engines caught fire and it force landed on the south coast somewhere.

They'd been sending us out here tooling around, two of us had been lost altogether and had to bale out, one over Cornwall and the other over East Anglia, and at last we'd got something but when I got down I think it was Brian Kingcome who was flight commander, he wasn't at all pleased. He said 'Why did you do that? We're not here to prance about in the night, we're day fighters and now they're going to go on sending us up and we won't get any joy' so that was disappointing but years later another chap had been writing his biography and mentioned this thing and he said at last somebody had succeeded and I thought after all these years I'd been vindicated.

Unlike Allan Wright, who had been trained as a day fighter pilot, Terry Clark, as an air gunner with 219 Squadron, had spent his time training for night fighting. His aircraft was a Bristol Blenheim, built as a fast light bomber in 1935, adapted as a night fighter and, by 1940, outpaced and outgunned by virtually every German aircraft it was supposed to shoot down.

When I joined 219 Squadron and I became operational I felt a great thrill. I felt this is what I've been trained to do. We were airborne at night and we used to patrol along the coast waiting for enemy action. I was ready with my machine gun to do my job as I had been trained. Night after night we would go up hoping that we would see something that we could engage and destroy.

The squadron was broken into two flights, B Flight would be on for two nights and then A Flight would go on for two nights and during the time you were off you would do more training and more German aircraft identification and visit searchlight units, just to get to know all the operational parts that went on even when you were in the air and I must admit as we went on month after month, and we were not getting any activity, I was beginning to wonder if I should ever fire at the enemy. He would have to be fairly close if he was going to do any damage and if he saw me first he'd probably wipe me out before I had my chance to do anything.

With the Blenheim, the mark 1 short nose Blenheim, I used to have the feeling that we weren't going to get very far. We really needed something faster and with more equipment than just machine guns. We had guns in the wings and

I had my gun but I felt that we were lacking and if we were really going to get down to night fighting we needed something better. We really were reliant on ground control giving us instructions and pointing us in the direction of the enemy. We did then go down to Redhill and that's when it all started.

219 Squadron was moved to RAF Redhill, in Surrey, In October 1940. Waiting for them was the first of the aircraft that was going to change the face of night fighting and give Terry Clark the aircraft he needed.

We were told we were converting to the Beaufighter. We'd never seen a Beaufighter and we didn't see one until we arrived down at Redhill. My first reaction was well where is the turret? There wasn't one, there wasn't going to be one. There wasn't going to be an air gunner. It was an AI operator, airborne interception, and the word radar came in. So I had to give up my air gunnery. All the air gunners objected and wanted to go to Bomber Command but we were not allowed to go because we knew about this AI so we had to retrain on the squadron and become operational immediately. I first thought, what a waste of time this is, but then when I got into it I could see this was going to be the answer. This was where we were going to get in touch with the enemy aircraft and do some damage because the Beaufighter was equipped with four 20mm cannons and that would certainly make the enemy cough and that was a thrill then. I felt that at last we were getting something to use that would really do the job.

We were still two crew. You were kept together because with AI you had to talk a picture. You had your AI equipment but from what you were looking at you had to talk to your pilot and describe what was going on, where the aircraft was, was it above or below, left or right, and was it getting closer. You had to create a picture by talking to the pilot so he could more or less know where the enemy aircraft was and that is why, once you were teamed up, you were kept with the same pilot. I kept the same pilot for three years and we got on like a house on fire. It was absolute teamwork together.

I had my perspex dome so I could see out into the night sky and he was up in his pilot's cockpit right up in the front. Between us were drums of ammunition. The four cannon were below my feet and it was my job, if he used up the ammunition, to take the old drums off and replace them rather like a powder monkey. Then we eventually got belt-fed cannon so that job ceased.

Some people sometimes wonder how on earth we ever made contact with the enemy but when you were scrambled the moment you were airborne you would be taken over by GCI, Ground Control Interceptor station. They had big radar that could see all that was going on in that area of the sky. I had radar that would only have a limitation of three miles and it would indicate to me whether an enemy aircraft was to my left or my right, above me or below me and then I would have the moment we got a contact. GCI would call us up and say they had business in our area and give us a course to steer towards the enemy. I would be watching my radar and the moment I got a contact the ground control station would then stop talking to us and it was then my conversation with my pilot, giving him instructions, that would eventually get him close to the enemy so that he could see it and then it was entirely up to him because he controlled the four cannons.

When we were night flying from Catterick I never realised that we were flying through the Battle of Britain and it wasn't until, I think, Winston Churchill made the statement that one realised there was such a thing as the Battle of Britain. We had no idea. We were just going up, doing as we were told, flying as we were told and doing our job. I don't think anybody had any idea how vital that was.

Terry would have to wait for his first success until April 1941. On one night, with Wing Commander Tom Pike as his pilot, he tracked and they destroyed two German bombers.

29 Squadron Blenheim 1F night fighter pilot, Peter Kells, climbs into his aircraft for a night patrol from Coleby Grange, Lincolnshire in October 1940

RAF

TO THE BITTER END

Almost as soon as the Battle of Britain was over, Air Chief Marshal Sir Hugh Dowding, Air Officer Commanding RAF Fighter Command was sacked from his post with what can only be described as indecent and spiteful haste.

In November of 1940, he was sacked by a single phone call and bluntly told 'The Air Council has no further work for you'. He was given just twenty-four hours to clear his desk and go. Described as 'almost blind with fatigue' from the effort of winning the Battle, and true to his own quiet nature, he made no protest and just went.

Before this though Hugh Dowding sent one last simple and heartfelt letter to all operational fighter stations and units. It read:

My dear Fighter Boys,

In sending you this, my last message, I wish I could say all that is in my heart. I cannot hope to surpass the simple eloquence of the Prime Minister's words, 'Never before has so much been owed by so many to so few." The debt remains and will increase.

In saying good-bye to you I want you to know how continually you have been in my thoughts, and that, though our direct connection may be severed, I may yet be able to help you in your gallant fight.

Good-bye to you and God bless you all.

Air Chief Marshal Hugh Dowding November 24th 1940

Air Vice Marshal Keith Park – commander of 11 Group and the man who had perhaps done more than any other to win the Battle of Britain – was also fired brutally and unceremoniously.

The reason given was that both men were essentially too defensive in their thinking, that they had disregarded the superior tactic of 'Big Wings' proposed by 12 Group commander Leigh-Mallory, and that neither had any answer to the bombing of London by night. In truth, Leigh-Mallory had the ear of important figures in government and Dowding and Park did not. It was Leigh-Mallory who now was rewarded by being given the plum job of commander of 11 Group, courtesy of the Air Minister Archibald Sinclair, of whom it was reliably said that he couldn't tell a Spitfire from a Hurricane and – on inspection visits – had no idea whether he was visiting an 11 or 12 Group station.

To add further insult to injury, attempts were made to write both men out of the official history of the battle. A 32 page booklet issued by the Air Ministry about the Battle of Britain failed to mention either man once.

Air Vice-Marshal Trafford Leigh-Mallory inspects the WAAF

Friends and colleagues

The core of a pilot's existence was the squadron. He lived, ate, partied, flew and died as part of a squadron. Here the pilots give a little of the flavour of being part of a close-knit team; leadership, making friends, working together, flying and fighting together and sometimes losing friends and colleagues.

Actually it was daunting because 32 Squadron was a well known front line Royal Air Force squadron with some excellent pilots and I was very humble as I realised I was only a number really because quite frankly I had not a clue, let's be honest about it. Coming straight from the training school to that, the squadron commander realised that because I think I only did about three trips with 32 and he said, to the three of us, 'You three sergeant pilots are useless. I can't have you here' and he sent us to Sutton Bridge to continue our training where we flew our Hurricanes in training. Some people might consider that we might have been depressed but I think the three of us were sensible enough to realise that we weren't going to last if we were carrying on in the front line at that time. We'd never fired a gun in our lives. We'd got no idea what to do really. Never been taught how to use our gunsights or anything like that and to be put into the front line, as the squadron commander realised, was ridiculous.

Tony Pickering

Comradeship. Love of one's fellow man. We lived hard, we played hard. It was just a question of not letting the bastards grind you down basically. It was an unforgettable collection of people and somehow they had an atmosphere about them. Many's the time I've gone straight to dispersal having been chucked out of the White Hart at Brasted or even gone up to a night club and gone straight to dispersal at three in the morning because we were on dawn readiness and one did that, parties most nights, pretty ladies around, we went to Manston after the battle and that was like a haven although Manston was as near to the French coast as its possible to get. The weather clamped while we were there and we used to go to a pub called the Fleur de Lis in Canterbury and I can see it now clearly, the chaps in this low, it was a very old, 13th Century pub, best brews, cigarette smoke rising to the ceiling, tinkling jewellery, comradeship, buying each other drinks and being together. Didn't want to go with anybody else, forget them, no other squadron except 92. Together we lived and fought and played very hard.

Geoffrey Wellum

I never really got intimate with any of these chaps. You know people have often said was it dreadful when you lost one of your friends and I would say well of course it was but they were only friends for a few weeks. I'd never met anyone in 605 until I went there in July and by September we'd lost some of them but we were really people passing in the night, if you like. It wasn't like old friendships where you'd known each other for years and years.

Bob Foster

You mainly flew your own aeroplane. I mean you had two different flights and if you could you stuck with your own aeroplane and you got to know the ground crew very well. You were on christian name terms with them all and they were very concerned when you landed. They said 'Have you fired all your ammunition, Sir?' You'd say yes and they'd be very pleased and they were extremely supportive and enthusiastic and got on very well. I thought the spirit of the whole station and specially down at the squadron was superb and that's one of the things that kept you going. Had they all been morose and under confident it would have affected your own morale but everybody was dead keen to get on with the job. They used to put your name on it and do various things and if you shot some aircraft down they would put the little crosses on and they were very, very supportive and very keen for you to do well.

John Ellacombe

The ground crew were part of the squadron. You were their pilot. You had a rapport with them. You gave them a bottle of whisky if you could get it as a Christmas present. You'd have a chat with them about their problems but they were always there and you'd see them, if they were waiting for someone to come back and they didn't turn up, you could see them looking out to the south, south east, and then when he didn't turn up they'd go and give a hand somewhere else, all the time aware. Mine, they were always waiting for me. The moment the aircraft stopped in dispersal they'd jump up on the wings, undo my straps, undo the door for me, help me out, all that sort of thing. 'Get anything today Sir?' 'No I sprayed bullets all over Kent.' 'What again?' This is a great thing about a fighter squadron in war. It's a very tight community from the ground crew who look after you, a fitter, a rigger, each aeroplane had its own, it was their aeroplane and you were permitted to fly it.

Geoffrey Wellum

My view of Victor Beamish was simply astonishing. I reckoned of about five men who were great leaders in the war he was certainly the first that I met. He was an inspirational man. He sort of oozed confidence. He was always very cheerful. He used to come and have a beer in the bar and he would chat to all the chaps and we liked him because he was a leader and he used to fly and join your squadron in combat. He was always very aggressive and very keen to get on with the job.

John Ellacombe

92 Squadron had a reputation. In fact I think we were known throughout Fighter Command as a load of playboys. Ill disciplined, red linings to our tunics and that sort of thing. Yes we had a bit of a reputation for being a bloody-minded lot. Well you see, in a way, it's understandable. We'd lost four COs who'd spent a couple of days in the chair, been shot down and then pushed off. And Brian did all the fighting and leading until October when Johnny Kent came. Now our attitude was here's a new chap, Johnny Kent, is he going to occupy the seat for three or four days and then push off somewhere? Or get killed? Or shot down? You know, let him adapt to us which was probably the wrong attitude but that's what it was and you can understand it. We'd been leaderless by which I mean a squadron without a leader, CO, since Dunkirk and Brian Kingcome was 92 Squadron and we'd follow him anywhere. Johnny Kent came along and tried to read the riot act which caused quite a lot of unhappiness but in the end we got used to each other and he became one of the boys and took us through into '41

Geoffrey Wellum

When we were in the air we were well looked after. You were a pilot and you were treated the same as an officer completely. On the ground, unfortunately, at Gravesend with all due respect to the British Army, the army fed the sergeant pilots, the officers were in the clubhouse and were fed by service men, RAF cooks and people like that. But we were fed by the army and quite frankly the food we were given, if I'd given it to pigs or sheep I'd have been in trouble because it was terrible. I'd never had food like it in my life but Squadron Leader Hogan realised what was going on and then every evening after we'd done our flying Squadron Leader Hogan realised we were not getting correct food and we had dinner every night in the Officers' mess, all the sergeant pilots were told to go to the Officers' mess and have dinner with the officers which actually gave us a good meal every day.

Tony Pickering

Well Joe Pegg was one of the original members who had flown with 610 down at Biggin Hill and elsewhere and he was a superb pilot and belonged to the old school. He seldom used the RT, did hand movements for everything which was great particularly if your RT at the moment was turned onto the IFF mode so you could neither hear or receive messages. We were flying one day in tight formation up the Northumberland coast, at virtually 25 feet hopping over groins and things like that. And on this occasion we were flying there – it takes a lot of concentration to fly tides at low level, he said "I don't want to distract you at all, don't move your eyes from where you're looking" he said "I'm going to read you an excerpt from a little book I've got." And I had a quick look and I could see him with this book held in his left hand and he was flying with his right hand. It was an extract from the Karma Sutra. He said "Are you enjoying this? I'll read some more", and he carried on. He was reading. At the same time he was watching, pulling up and eventually he said "Well I think we're a little too near the station now for me to read anymore particularly." We'd had about 20 minutes of this. Bloody marvellous, he really was.

David Denchfield

We went up to Church Fenton for a while and then suddenly my friend and I were posted to Bader who was at Coltishall but operating from Duxford. We got a very cool response because I don't think Bader liked sergeant pilots. He seemed to believe, for some reason, that all pilots should be commissioned and we got a very curt greeting and more or less told to go off to the sergeants' mess until we were sent for. We weren't sent for for a long time so I became quite good at snooker. It was the first time we had come across this class distinction, not in the squadron itself but in the sergeants mess because the old sweats, the sergeants and warrant officers thought that we were far too young to be in the sergeants mess. They made life as difficult as they could but anyway we got over that eventually. Bader had a lot of pain from the stumps of his legs and

I've seen him sitting on the side of a bed in dispersal where he's taken his legs off and I had a look at his stumps and they were red raw. He was lashing talcum powder on them and doing them up again. He'd put his legs on and off he'd go. He had a marvellous method for scrambling because he had his ground crew really trained. They knew where he was at and what to do, where to lift him, where to pull him and how to do his straps. He was a good man, he certainly had guts.

Doug Nicholls

Well in a funny way I think you'll understand when I say I stopped making friends and that sums it up because I had too many friends killed and you did have to stop. You get used to having friends around you and suddenly they're not there. You see the chap who was there at breakfast is killed an hour later and you never see him any more. It sounds awfully easy to say that now but to us, we were only young kids, 20...in our twenties. Early twenties many of us. We'd lost too many friends and I stopped making friends.

Dennis David

We used to practice dogfights. Two were killed whilst I was there and on both occasions I was flying with them. On one we were night flying in Spitfires which was the most hazardous thing I ever did. It was a terrifying experience, we were in complete blackout, no horizon whatsoever, the exhaust red hot and you spent all your time looking at instruments to keep the right way up. I was flying with one chap at night in our Spitfires and for some extraordinary reason he dived straight into the ground and was killed. They never knew why or how he did it but on another occasion I was practicing dogfighting with a chap during the day and for some reason he did the same thing, simply crashed straight into the ground and was killed. Extraordinary. I had one very narrow escape when I was training. We used to take each other up in Harvards and I was a passenger with a chap called Woods and he was shooting up the house of a girlfriend, diving down and pulling out and I was terrified as the passenger in the back. Anyway I survived but the next day he was doing precisely the same thing with another pilot when he pulled out too quickly, the plane stalled and they both were killed. It could have been me the day before.

William Walker

I think most blokes were in the same boat even though, when you think of it, some of the chaps we had in 151 had fought in France and at Dunkirk and they had been flying on operations for a long time. They had all already got DFCs or DFCs and bars, they had shot down a lot of aeroplanes and been in all sorts of things and the one chap who saddened me in many ways was Teddy Donaldson, my first CO because he had reached the stage where he didn't fly again in the whole war. He was so shattered and been damaged and of course he was actually shot down on one occasion and landed in the sea and he was in the water for several hours before he was picked up so there was one of the blokes, one of the outstanding pilots, who's nerve had actually gone and, you know, realised that somehow you are determined not to show fear. It was a difficult thing to describe but I suppose its the same as facing a fast bowler when they're bowling 90mph at you. You are determined 'I'm not going to be frightened.'

John Ellacombe

By the time we'd got to Manston we'd got through quite a lot of people. It seemed to ease off a bit towards the beginning of the October November period. Most of the big fights, big combats, had gone. They'd stopped their bomber offensive. Chaps were still getting picked off because 109s used to come over very high, drop a bomb any old where and then do a sweep round while you were climbing up to them so they had a height advantage. But you had no option. You put it behind you and you didn't think about it. You know you might in a more sombre moment be in the pub having a pint and say 'Cheers mate.' You missed absent friends but you accepted it. You had no option. It would drive you nuts if you did. It was stiff upper lip stuff

Geoffrey Wellum

Eddie Egan and I were young fellows of a similar nature, similar education in the squadron, two young sergeant pilots who used to read books, play music, go and have a half pint and mix with the girls but we lived a similar sort of life. We were probably two lads from a village in the country who'd lived a sheltered life, ex-grammar school boys. Not used to the rough and tumble of civilian life and we got on well together. Of course he was shot down flying alongside me. We were flying together and what I thought were Spitfires came down and picked him off but they weren't, they were 109s and it was too late. I never knew why they picked him and not me. Because they could have got me the same because we

RAF pilots listen to their New Zealand officer (right) as he tells them how he baled out after dogfighting with the enemy on 16 August 1940 *both thought they were Spitfires. We'd been talking to each other. We'd been split up from the squadron, told what to do to get back into the squadron again, fly to a certain position at a certain height. We were both endeavouring to do that but these 109s picked him off.*

TONY PICKERING

I did attend one funeral during Dunkirk and then it was stopped because quite rightly they reckoned it wouldn't do morale any good and I thoroughly approved of that. I lost my best friend in the very beginning and I was deeply affected that evening, that night but then the next morning you just carried on. Sometimes people came and went and you hardly knew them.

ALLAN WRIGHT

I think squadron life taught you that you really can't operate as an individual. You've got to be a member of a team whatever you're doing. Whether you're in engineering, or banking, whether you're in the law you're a member of a team and you've got to work together. You've got to realise that there are always people working with you who have the capabilities. They are older, more experienced. You've got to learn to give and take and that's what I think squadron life taught me in the air force. We were part of a team and you must always work as part of a team.

TONY PICKERING

Who Won?

It was obvious to all that the RAF had won the Battle of Britain by the end of September 1940. The nation had not meekly surrendered when the Germans turned on it. The RAF had maintained air superiority in the skies over England and consequently Hitler had been forced to postpone his invasion plans indefinitely. Far from collapsing from attrition, the RAF was actually growing stronger, more hard-hitting and more effective while the Luftwaffe were weakening and even perhaps afraid now of the consequences of launching bombing raids by day.

The air battle had been very evenly matched. The RAF had lost 1,087 planes and 481 pilots. 357 Spitfires had been shot down, together with 601 Hurricanes. The Luftwaffe had lost 1,652 aircraft and just over 3,000 pilots and air crew. Of the aircraft lost 778 were bombers. 533 Bf 109s were shot down.

The deciding factor in the campaign was most probably the decision to switch from bombing RAF airfields and radar installations in favour of the terror bombing of London. The decision – an act of high dudgeon by Hitler and Goering after the bombing of Berlin – gave the RAF vital time to repair their defences, re-equip and strengthen. It has been estimated that the RAF was just 24 hours from defeat when the pressure on them was finally eased.

There were of course many other factors that had a direct effect on the outcome. The Luftwaffe, for all its efforts, was simply the wrong sort of air force to fight this sort of campaign. It was designed to provide close air support to the army, not to get locked into a bloody and prolonged battle of attrition. It had no heavy four engined bombers either, making it something of a lightweight in striking capabilities, and no long range fighters. No one had ever foreseen the need.

It was also, all too often, flying blind. German intelligence was exceptionally poor, even to the extent that they couldn't understand the structure and group breakdown of the RAF. This meant that the Luftwaffe often bombed the wrong targets, including airfields not involved in the

Spitfires of 609 Squadron ready for action at Middle Wallop in Hampshire

PR
O

Battle of Britain, and aircraft factories not building the fighters the RAF so desperately needed. What's more, they could not estimate with any accuracy either the quantity of British aircraft available for the fight nor the number of pilots. In one week in mid-August, German Intelligence confidently estimated Fighter Command had 300 serviceable aircraft at their disposal. In reality, they had 700. Underestimating RAF strength so gravely sent a genuine (and deeply demoralising) shock through the Luftwaffe when – contrary to expectations - they encountered such strong resistance to their raids in mid-September. While both sides had claimed far more combat victories than had actually occurred, the Germans attempt to keep a tally of the number of RAF aircraft they'd destroyed was so inaccurate that it actually amounted to more aircraft than the RAF actually had.

Goering himself was another determining factor in the German defeat. He was a man from another age, his knowledge of aerial combat was gained during the Great War. New developments, such as radar, baffled him and what he couldn't understand or appreciate, he tended to underestimate or ignore in his arrogance. This meant he did not prioritise the destruction of radar stations sufficiently. If he had, he could have largely blinded the RAF. The Observer Corp warnings would have been greatly inferior. Goering was also a deeply flawed individual. At the start of the conflict he was respected and even loved by the majority of his aircrews who possessed a deep loyalty to him. However, as the Battle of Britain progressed and things did not go the way he had envisaged, he began to turn on his men accusing them of being cowards, incompetents and worse. To men locked in a daily life or death struggle and suffering terrifying casualties, this was simply unbearable and they turned against him. Goering desperately wanted his men to nickname him 'The Iron Man'. Instead, by the end of the Battle of Britain they were openly calling him 'Fatty'.

Goering of course was only one reason for the poisonous decline in Luftwaffe morale by the end of September. Casualty rates were another. As the Battle moved deeper North over England to encompass London, Luftwaffe bomber crews had to fly further into enemy territory. They encountered stronger resistance, were usually under attack for longer and could count on less protection from their fighter escorts. The relatively fresh 12 Group could now get at them in addition to the badly mauled 11 Group. Bailing out or crash-landing, they had no chance of escape to fight again and surviving crews saw fewer and fewer of their comrades return. And, quite simply, many were bone weary from three months of frontline combat duties. Many had been shot down in the Channel more than once and were wondering now when their luck would run out. As the weeks dragged on with the invasion effectively cancelled, many simply could not understand what they were risking everything for. Many increasingly suspected – with some justification – that they were little more than fighter-bait. Meanwhile, the fighter pilots had been harangued and ridiculed by Goering to such an extent that they were by the end close to losing all motivation.

For the British, the use of radar had enabled fighters to be vectored to where they were needed with a good degree of accuracy and Dowding's quite brilliant if parsimonious use of minimum force conserved the fighter force for just long enough. The introduction of fresh pilots in the form of two Polish and one Czech Squadron in late August-early September added a new effectiveness to RAF interception just when it was needed most. Although fresh these pilots were not raw or novices. They were men already hardened in air combat over their homelands or over France – and were fierce with a desire for revenge. They hated the enemy with a passion not usually matched by British fighter pilots and fought with a ferocity that rattled their opponents. They may well have tipped the balance in the RAF's favour at the critical moment.

The RAF too enjoyed a boost from the air war shifting away from the Channel and over London. More pilots survived being shot down and returned swiftly to their units to fight again – some within a matter of just hours. More pilots meant more fighters in the air – and Britain had managed to keep the production of new aircraft fast enough to replace the machines lost. Aircraft production numbers were incredibly consistent throughout the battle at around 460 machines a month despite increased German targeting of the production plants. RAF morale increased consequently, aided further by a sense that they were now winning the air war.

Some point to the swift dismissal of both Dowding and Park shortly after the Battle of Britain was finished as evidence of some deep flaw in RAF fighter tactics and that the battle should have been won with much more ease, but this is deeply misleading. The sackings were due almost entirely to personal and political infighting in the Air Ministry and RAF High Command coupled with the RAF's understandable difficulty in intercepting German bombers by night. Both Park and Dowding performed quite exceptionally. They understood that the Luftwaffe were waging a campaign of attrition and were counting on fighting a very few but decisive mass air engagements. They denied them this, sending up interceptors sparingly and avoiding marauding German formations that were largely comprised of fighters. They also understood how fighting over the Channel led to high pilot losses and tried to pull the air war further north and away from the coast to help reduce casualties. Tactics were under constant review and refined throughout the fighting – one such example being the decision to vector Hurricanes against bomber formations and Spitfires against their fighter escorts wherever possible.

Hurricane production at the Gloster factory in Hucclecotte

Behind the scenes, Dowding did a magnificent job in supporting Park by somehow almost magicking new pilots out of thin air for him, while ensuring he always had sufficient fighter aircraft for them to fly. The communications network that he and Park had largely devised during the interwar years worked well when called upon and their support for the Hurricane and Spitfire paid genuine dividends.

Britain's victory in the Battle of Britain was quite certainly more important than Hitler realised at the time. He never seemed to have set his heart on an invasion, and would certainly have preferred a British capitulation to the merest threat of invasion by weak and appeasing politicians. He may well never have expected to have to invade. At the end of October 1940, he did not acknowledge – or accept - that Germany had just suffered its first major defeat of the war. Britain was still at bay as far as he was concerned, hammered by night by his bombers and slowly strangled and deprived of vital supplies out in the Atlantic by his U-Boat Wolf Packs, who referred to this period of the war as 'The Happy Time'. Even today, Germany still does not pay too much attention or attach too much importance to the events of July-October 1940. Back then, Hitler simply turned his attention East to deal with those who he truly despised, laying plans for a summer invasion of Soviet Russia.

In Britain too, there was no sense of having achieved any victory that would change the war – just some sense of relief. Britain had defeated the threat of invasion, but the Blitz still raged and the convoys were still being sunk. Churchill was forced to fight back and look for victories for now in the Middle East and even there, fortunes ebbed and flowed. However, what the Battle of Britain had achieved was a new sense of determination in Britain to fight on. After nine months of a phoney war and strong resistance to war from both politicians and civilians, Britain was now blooded, roused and fully motivated in its fight against the Nazis.

In their resistance to Nazism, the British were still virtually alone in the winter of 1940. America looked on and some admired the nation's pluck. Many were horrified and disgusted by the persistent terror bombing of London but its citizenry were still very opposed to the idea of going to war in Britain's defence. The large German and Irish communities were hostile to Britain and largely preferred to support Germany, while the American political left hated Britain's perceived imperialism and actually saw Hitler as a leader they could potentially work with because he had worked together with Stalin to carve up Poland. If Stalin was friends with Hitler he had to be the horse to back, they reasoned. 1941 was to give them something of a shock.

Over the next year, the American economy benefitted from selling materials to Britain to aid the war effort, to the point that the trade nearly wrecked the British economy, but they stayed resolutely neutral. It took Pearl Harbor and Hitler's declaration of war on America to finally bring them into the fight. When they did, they found Britain still free to use as 'an aircraft carrier off the coast of Europe' and then as a base for the invasion of Occupied Europe - and that perhaps, was the greatest legacy and reward of the Battle of Britain.

Tower Bridge stands out against a backdrop of smoke & fires

Pilots look back

Below these pilots share their reflections on the Battle of Britain. These are some of their lasting memories of those momentous months of the Summer of 1940.

Like an automaton. In the end you didn't think about it. You were tired. I can always see dawn readiness. I can see Spitfires standing in the gloom at dispersal. I can hear the airmen and the clank of petrol bowsers and I can remember sort of looking up at the sky and thinking 'oh, it's going to be a lovely day again, oh God, another dawn.' Said a little prayer, 'it's going to be another busy day. If I forget you don't forget me. Just give me this day, please just give me this day.'

Geoffrey Wellum

The good fellowship between pilots in the squadron was something that was absolutely unique. Any one of us would have done anything for anybody else. They were probably the closest knit company of people I will ever find in all my life. It was the feeling between pilots that was something very special and something very precious.

William Walker

You decide early on you're either going to survive or you're not. And if you don't survive you can't worry about it as there's no point so you coped that way. There were times when you'd think "I've got away with it so far, probably tomorrow I'll get killed' that cropped up in your mind now and again but have a drink and forget it...and we drank quite a lot during the war.

Pete Brothers

August...I suppose it was the most exciting, frightening, invigorating period of my life. When you think how many blokes were shot down, in that three week period we had six killed, eight wounded and eleven others had baled out or force landed. When you think over that period Frank Marlow, our intelligence officer, kept the records and showed we had destroyed 35 German aeroplanes in that three weeks so you take your losses and account what the Germans had and it was really quite astonishing.

John Ellacombe

I think the main thing, if you live in the UK, it's the only thing that happened over England so therefore it's very personal to people here. What happened in Malta and the Middle East is something a long way away and so if you're having an air show at Biggin Hill you obviously concentrate on the Battle of Britain and the two aeroplanes in the battle were the Hurricane and the Spitfire. You don't see poor old Defiants there. You don't see any Blenheims there which did part of this. For the first 20 or 30 years after the war nobody wanted to know anything about it. We had our association and there was always Battle of Britain Day on 15 September, but there wasn't all this emphasis that there has been over the last 20 or 30 years when people started writing books about it and then they made a film about it, Battle of Britain, in 1969, and now it's become a, not a myth, but it's been brought forward as the definitive battle, which it probably was. I think that's another thing, to us the battle went on, but it did have an effect on the rest of the war. Had we lost this thing, had the Germans either invaded or bombed us to oblivion we wouldn't be here now.

Bob Foster

I think the legend has grown since the war. I don't think at the time any of us realised that the Battle of Britain would be remembered in quite such a way. One considered oneself as just lucky to have joined Fighter Command. I had the greatest admiration for the 'Bomber Boys'. I think they deserve far more credit than they've been given and certainly more than the fighter boys. The idea of setting off on a flight to Berlin in a Lancaster, one pilot, because there was only one pilot, there was no dual control in a Lancaster. The long journey there for hours on end and arriving over Berlin having fought off enemy fighters on the way, arrive at Berlin to be shot by artillery and fighter aircraft and then drop your bombs and fly all the way home on a trip that lasted sometimes ten hours? That is bravery. Fighter pilots were up and down so quickly that you didn't have time to think. The longest time we spent in a Spitfire was in convoy patrols. We could just stay up for two hours on light mixture but normally we were never up for longer than an hour.

William Walker

You never thought for a moment you would lose it. You became aware that you were denying them their aim. I always had great satisfaction if I saw a formation of Dorniers, I remember one evening Dorniers jettisoning their bombs. You'd stopped them getting to London or wherever it was they were going, jettisoning their bombs over open countryside. They weren't particular, these chaps, if they saw a little village and they were getting hammered they would jettison over it, it wouldn't matter, but that I found very satisfactory that you denied them their aim because for the first time their aim had been denied them. They had not achieved what they set out to do. In fact, in spite of the self styled intellectuals and visionaries of today we defeated them, we beat them and we stopped them doing what they wanted to do.

GEOFFREY WELLUM

I never thought the battle was lost, no, damn difficult, and how long is this supposed to go on? Do we spend the rest of the war doing this? I didn't know, of course, the effect of casualties on either side. We seemed to have more people coming along. The Germans kept going, how were we to know? But it did cross my mind that I didn't think I'd be able to cope with this for a year or two. Then I think we knew we'd won because I was there from September onwards so the whole of that month was very active. I was shot down and in hospital for about a month and came back in October and by then there were practically no bombers but just 109s coming over with a bomb each, well that was obviously different and I thought well this is Winter and I suppose they're getting their people together to have another good go next Summer.

ALLAN WRIGHT

Well we all got tired, I'll say that much. I've never forgotten one Saturday evening round about the end of September, I suppose, when Dowding put up about 12 squadrons on the Saturday evening. There wasn't a hun in sight. I don't think the hun had left their aerodromes in France. It was later in the year and about an hour before dusk. We flew up and down, these squadrons, on the railway line between Ashford in Kent and up towards Croydon, there's a stretch of straight railway line. We would patrol that line quite often and he put these squadrons up on either side of this line and everywhere you went you saw a squadron of Hurricanes, a squadron of Spitfires...just on that one occasion I felt the morale of the squadron was getting a bit low, we'd taken punishment and morale leapt up immediately when you could see nothing but your own fighters all over, squadron there, squadron here, and I've never forgotten it. I don't know the date of it but I know it was a Saturday, for some reason I have never forgotten it was a Saturday evening, and I've never seen that written in a book anywhere, no-one's ever mentioned it to me but I do remember it vividly. Certainly my morale had gone down and I felt that it had for a lot of us. We'd received a hammering, we'd lost a lot of people but on that Saturday night, in my opinion, that's when Dowding really showed himself. He put us up and we could see nothing, we had about three quarters of an hour of flying, and there was nothing but Spitfires and Hurricanes to be seen all in beautiful squadron form, all tightly together and then we landed and I don't think the hun crossed the coast. That was a magnificent move on the part of Dowding.

TONY PICKERING

John Gard'ner, then a Pilot Officer, in front of his Defiant on his return to 141 Squadron in early 1941

Sergeant Terry Clark with 219 squadron. Top Row, fourth from right

John Ellacombe shows off his shredded trousers kept as a souvenir after his stay in hospital

Wing Commander Bob Foster DFC, AFC

Bob Foster was born in South London in 1920 and after leaving school he worked for Shell-Mex BP. He joined the RAFVR in March 1939 and with his employers generously giving him two months paid leave of absence Bob went to learn to fly. Bob completed his flying training on Hurricanes at Grantham and was posted to 605 Squadron at Drem in Scotland. 605 was sent south to Croydon on 7 September arriving in the early evening when he could see London's docks in flames to the east. Bob destroyed or damaged a number of German aircraft during the Battle of Britain and was still with the squadron when the battle ended. Posted to 54 Squadron he went to Australia and spent the next two years defending Darwin against the Japanese before returning to England. Joining the newly formed RAF Public Relations unit Bob accompanied journalists in the weeks before D-Day, went to Normandy soon afterwards and personally witnessed the destruction of Caen by RAF Bomber Command. In July he was the first British officer into Paris and, by chance, took part in General de Gaulle's liberation procession through the city. After the war Bob rejoined Shell-Mex BP and stayed with them until retirement in 1975. A keen supporter of the Battle of Britain Fighter Association he became chairman in 2009 until he passed away in July 2014.

Squadron Leader Doug Nicholls DFC

Doug Nicholls was born in 1919 and became a pre-war RAFVR pilot. In June 1940 he converted to Hurricanes and flew during the Battle of Britain with 85 and 242 Squadrons. In September he joined 151 Squadron at Digby and on 30 September he shared in the destruction of a Ju 88 and returned to Digby with his Hurricane severely damaged by enemy fire. Later in the war he flew Hurricanes with 258 Squadron in the Far East from Singapore. On 10 February 1942 the three surviving Hurricanes of 258 were withdrawn to Palembang with Doug being one of the nine pilots evacuated from Java to Ceylon. He took part in the defence of Colombo and flew intensively in Burma in 1944. After the war Doug became a teacher, and also instructed at No 22 Air Training Corps Gliding School. In 1960 Doug took his family to Uganda and later Botswana. He returned to Britain after Idi Amin expelled Uganda's Asians in 1972 and taught at schools in Grimsby. He made his last flight on his 80th birthday in a Tiger Moth, taking the controls and executing a turn, at Sywell in Northamptonshire. Doug Nicholls passed away on 6 December 2014.

Squadron Leader Geoffrey Wellum DFC

Born in London in 1921 Geoffrey Wellum joined the Royal Air Force straight from school. In May 1940, in the heat of the Dunkirk air battles, he was posted to 92 Squadron to learn how to fly Spitfires. 92's CO, Roger Bushell, who would later become famous as one of the leaders of the Great Escape, was ready to send him back for more training but he was shot down that day and Geoffrey stayed. In September 1940 he saw his first action and his first kill, a Heinkel He 111. There were further claims during the hardest months of the battle and Geoffrey remained with the squadron until February 1942 when he was transferred to 65 Squadron. On 11 August 1942, he led eight Spitfires launched from the carrier HMS Furious to reinforce the fighter compliment on Malta. Here he joined 1435 Squadron on air defence duties before being rested. He had flown without a break for almost three years and was suffering from severe combat fatigue after three years intensive flying. He returned from Malta, becoming a test pilot on the Hawker Typhoon, and finished the war as a gunnery instructor. Post war Geoffrey stayed in the RAF until 1961 before retiring and working in the city of London. His memoir First Light, which he never intended to be for publication, became a bestseller for Penguin. He died on July 18 2018.

Air Commodore John Ellacombe CB, DFC*

John Ellacombe was born in Northern Rhodesia in 1920. He came to England and joined the RAF in 1939 and was posted to 151 Squadron in July 1940, immediately converting to Hurricanes. Right in the front line during the Battle of Britain John shot down a number of enemy aircraft and was shot down twice himself, the second time, in flames, he baled out and spent several months recovering from severe burns. He rejoined 151 Squadron, now a night fighter unit, before being posted to 253 Squadron flying alongside Turbinlite Havocs. He was shot down for a third time, in 1942, while attacking an enemy ground battery during the Dieppe operation. Converting to the Mosquito John joined 487(NZ) Squadron. During the D-Day and Normandy operations he was attacking targets such as V1 sites, roads and railways in support of ground operations. Postwar he had a long and successful career in the RAF which included being CO of 1 Squadron on Meteors, service in Aden, the USA, Bahrain and the UK. He retired from the RAF in 1973 and became a senior figure at St Thomas's hospital in London. A keen sportsman all his life John played golf until he was 88. John Ellacombe sadly passed away in May 2014 aged 94.

Flight Lieutenant William Walker AE

William Walker was born in Hampstead in 1913 and joined the RAFVR in September 1938 when, officially, he was too old to join up. Like so many others he was called up on 1 September 1939 and became a fighter pilot. He was posted to 616 Squadron at Leconfield in Yorkshire in June 1940. Soon after taking part in an attack against a major German raid on the north of England the squadron moved south to Kenley. On 26 August the squadron was attacked over the Channel and William's Spifire was hit. Wounded in the ankle he baled out at 20,000 ft taking a long time to land in the sea. Landing near a shipwreck he stayed afloat until picked up by a fishing boat. Suffering from hypothermia he was taken to hospital. When recovered William joined an aircraft ferry unit and then 116 Squadron. At the end of the war William was released from the RAF and rejoined the brewery trade, rising to become chairman of Ind Coope. William Walker died at the age of 99 in 2012, at the time the oldest surviving Battle of Britain veteran. His poetry, which he would recite annually at the service of remembrance at Capel-le-Ferne, was published in 2011 with all proceeds donated to the Battle of Britain Memorial Trust.

GROUP CAPTAIN DENNIS DAVID CBE, DFC*, AFC

Dennis David was born in July 1918. He joined the Reserves in 1937 and was sent to France with 87 Squadron on the outbreak of war aged 21. He became one of the highest-scoring RAF pilots of the Second World War, scoring an amazing 11 combat victories in May 1940, before the Battle of Britain had even begun. By the time the squadron was pulled back to Britain towards the end of May, he had won the DFC and Bar. Dennis continued to fly with 87 Squadron from Exeter during the Battle of Britain before being posted as a flight commander to 213 Squadron. His final kill was on October 19 when he shot down a Ju88 to bring his score to 20. In November he was posted to No 152, a Spitfire squadron. He spent two years instructing until, in 1943, he was sent to North Africa to command 89 Squadron, equipped with night-fighting Beaufighters. In 1944 he was promoted to group captain and posted to the Burma theatre. Dennis remained in the Far East after the war, and was in charge of Allied air operations in Java. He returned to the desert in 1948 to command El Adem but halfway through this posting he went as air attaché to Hungary. While he was there, the political situation deteriorated, and in October 1956 erupted into open revolt. Subsequent postings included the command of RAF Tangmere, from where he had flown during the Battle of Britain. He left the RAF in May 1967 and became an adviser to films such as The Battle of Britain and Aces High. He died on 25 August 2000.

FLIGHT LIEUTENANT TERRY CLARK DFM, AE

Terry Clark was born in Croydon on 11 April 1919. He joined 615 Squadron RAuxAF in March 1938 in Kenley and was called up in 1939, flying as a gunner in Hawker Hectors before being posted to 219 Sqn in July 1940 on Blenheims during the Battle of Britain. In September 1940, the squadron converted to Beaufighters and Terry retrained as a radar specialist. His job was to track enemy aircraft and guide the pilot towards the selected contact. It was while flying the Beaufighter that he was awarded the DFM on 8 July 1941 after assisting his pilot to shoot down three aircraft at night. He joined 1455 Flight in 1941 at Tangmere with Turbinlite Havocs, then flew the same aircraft with 1451 Flight at Hunsdon, locating enemy aircraft by Radar in the Havoc for accompanying fighters to attack and destroy. Terry was commissioned in 1942 and in May 1943 he was posted to No.488 (NZ) Squadron on the Mosquito. Terry was released from the RAF in 1945 and returned to civilian life. He died on 7 May 2020.

WARRANT OFFICER DAVID DENCHFIELD

David Denchfield was born in November 1919. Joining the RAFVR in May 1939 he was called up in November, soon after his 20th birthday. He took his first flight in a Spitfire and joined 610 Squadron at Acklington in October. Moved down to Westhampnett, a satellite station of Tangmere, he began sweeps across to France in early 1941. On a Blenheim escort to St Omer in February 1941 his aircraft was hit and, having baled out at 5,000 feet, he was captured by the Germans. He spent time in several POW camps, including Stalag Luft III, and at the end of the war in May 1945 flew back to the UK in a Lancaster of 617 Squadron. After the war David became a draughtsman and engineer. On retirement he and his family settled in Cambridgeshire. Sadly he passed away on 5 December 2012.

WING COMMANDER TERENCE KANE

Terence Kane joined the RAF in July 1938 on a short service commission. During his flying training he was injured in an Audax crash and admitted to hospital, however he was able to complete his training. After instructing he went to 7 OTU in July 1940, converted to Spitfires and joined 234 Squadron in September. He shared in the destruction of a Ju88 on the 22nd but the next day he failed to return from a routine patrol. His Spitfire was damaged in combat off the French coast and he baled out at 6,000 feet. Finally opening his parachute Terence reckoned he was three seconds away from hitting the sea as he came out of cloud. He was picked up from the sea and captured by the Germans. He was freed from POW camp in May 1945 and stayed in the RAF until 1950. He rejoined the RAF in April 1954, serving in the Fighter Control Branch, and retired in 1974. He died on 5 August 2016.

SQUADRON LEADER KEITH LAWRENCE DFC

Keith Lawrence was born in New Zealand in November 1919. He enrolled in the Civil Reserve of Pilots in February 1938 and successfully applied for a short serve commission in the RAF. Keith left for the UK in February 1939 . After training he joined the newly-formed 234 Squadron at Leconfield in November, initially on Blenheims but subsequently on Spitfires in March 1940. Keith's Battle of Britain started before the official date when he shared in the destruction of a Junkers Ju88 on 8 July, the squadron's first victory. Further victories followed before the squadron was withdrawn and Keith was posted to 603 Squadron at Hornchurch. In October he was posted to 421 Flight. During a weather recce on 26 November he was shot down. His Spitfire disintegrated but he found himself falling clear. He was picked up by a minesweeper and taken to Ramsgate, where he was admitted to hospital with his right arm dislocated and his right leg broken. Keith rejoined the squadron in January 1942 but soon afterwards was posted to Malta. Keith joined 185 Squadron at Hal Far, fighting through one of the most intense periods in the defence of Malta. He was promoted and took command of 185 leading the squadron until early August 1942. Various instructing posts followed before he returned to operations in February 1945 when he joined 124 Squadron at Manston. After the war Keith returned to New Zealand. He died on June 2 2016.

Squadron Leader Tony Pickering

Tony Pickering was born in Leicestershire in August 1920 and became an engineering apprentice in Rugby. Joining the RAFVR in 1939 Tony was called up and after training was sent to 32 Squadron on Hurricanes at Biggin Hill. After just a few days, together with two friends who also lacked the necessary experience, he was sent for further training. On his first flight in a Hurricane he had been told to make sure his gun button was off, just in case he got excited and shot down his flight commander! Returning to the squadron in August he was immediately posted to 501 Squadron at Gravesend, flying and fighting with them until the end of the battle. In September Tony was shot down, baled out and landed in the Guards depot at Caterham in Surrey. Later that month he took part in the destruction of an Me110 and then shot down an Me109 in October. After the battle Tony was posted to 601 Squadron before becoming an instructor. He then joined 131 Squadron as a flight commander before ending the war in the Middle East as a squadron commander. Leaving the RAF Tony returned to Rugby and continued with his engineering, eventually designing steam turbines and travelling the world. He died on March 24 2019.

Air Commodore Pete Brothers CBE, DSO, DFC*

Pete Brothers was born in Prestwich in 1917 and learned to fly at the age of 16. He joined the RAF in 1936 and flew Gloster Gauntlets with 32 Squadron. He first saw action in 1940 when as a flight commander, still with 32 Squadron based at Biggin Hill. He took part in the Battle of France, the Dunkirk air battles and the Battle of Britain, some of the most intensive fighting periods of the whole war. Awarded the DFC, he was transferred to the hard-hit 257 Squadron where he joined Bob-Stanford Tuck as a flight commander, restoring the inexperienced pilots' confidence. After a period of instructing he was promoted to Squadron Leader and took command of 457 Squadron RAAF, equipped with Spitfires. In time for the Dieppe operation in 1942, Pete took command of 602 Squadron followed by becoming Wing Leader of the Tangmere Wing, succeeding his old friend, Douglas Bader. By the end of the war Pete had amassed 875 operational hours over a 44-month period. He was credited with having personally shot down 16 enemy aircraft and damaged many more. He later went on to command 57 Squadron during the Malaya campaign and on his return to the UK Pete joined the V-Force, flying Valiant jet bombers. He retired in 1973. Pete Brothers died in December 2008.

Squadron Leader Cyril Bamberger DFC*, AE*

Cyril 'Bam' Bamberger was born in Cheshire in 1919 and volunteered for the Auxiliary Air Force in 1936. 610 Squadron, which would be his fighter squadron for most of the Battle of Britain, was a bomber squadron when 'Bam' joined as a photographer. However, after pilot training he returned to 610 and this time it was equipped with Spitfires. When 610 Squadron was withdrawn in September 'Bam' was posted to 41 Squadron and stayed with them until the end of the battle. Volunteering for Malta he joined 261 Squadron, this time on Hurricanes, and then went to 93 Squadron in Tunisia and subsequently back to Malta in 1943. He was awarded a DFC in 1943 and a bar a year later. Leaving the RAF in 1946 he returned to business but when 610 Squadron was reformed as a Royal Auxiliary Air Force unit again 'Bam' converted to Meteors, rejoined the squadron as a flight commander and eventually became CO. During the Korean War he was recommissioned into the RAF and served in intelligence eventually retiring in 1959. Cyril Bamberger passed away in 2008 aged 88

Wing Commander Tom Neil DFC*, AFC, AE

Tom 'Ginger' Neil was born in Bootle in 1920 and joined the RAFVR in 1938. Called up on the outbreak of war Tom completed his training and was posted to 249 Squadron flying Hurricanes. Based at North Weald 249 was in the front line for most of the Battle of Britain. In just three weeks in September alone Tom claimed five and two shared victories but in November his Hurricane collided with that of Wing Commander Victor Beamish and he was forced to bale out. In May 1941 he went with the squadron to Malta, flying his Hurricane off HMS Ark Royal, and by the time he returned in December 1941 he had achieved a total of 12 victories with four shared. In January 1944 Tom was attached as a liaison officer with 100th Fighter Wing of the US 9th Air Force where he flew Mustangs and took part in many ground attack sorties in Europe. In March 1945 Tom was posted to Burma, again flying Hurricanes, this time with No.1 Wing Indian Air Force. After the war he undertook a number of staff and operational postings before retiring in 1964. In civilian life Tom worked first in the USA and then as a director in the shoe industry, settling in Norfolk. Since retirement Tom has written six books based on his wartime experiences. He died on 11 July 2018.

Flight Lieutenant Jimmy Corbin DFC

Jimmy Corbin was a 'Man of Kent', born in Maidstone in 1917. Either side of the war Corbin was a teacher but always had a great interest in flying. Volunteering for the RAFVR in April 1939 Jimmy was called up at the outbreak of war. Following training, and with just 29 hours flying experience on a Spitfire, Jimmy was posted to 66 Squadron but due to his lack of experience his CO sent him north for further training. Rejoining the squadron Jimmy fought throughout the last weeks of the battle from Gravesend. Athol Forbes, the CO of 66 Squadron, decided, as the battle was coming to a close, that ten of the squadron's pilots should record their memories of the battle. Ten Fighter Boys was published in 1942 and included Jimmy Corbin's recollections but by that time half the contributors were dead,. After a year of almost continuous action Jimmy became an instructor before a posting to 72 Squadron in North Africa. At the end of the campaign he was awarded a DFC. He left the RAF at the end of the war but continued flying with the RAF Reserve. In 2010 Jimmy wrote his own memoirs, entitled Last of the Ten Fighter Boys. Jimmy Corbin died in 2012 aged 95.

Group Captain Billy Drake DSO, DFC*

Billy Drake was born in London in 1917 and christened Billy rather than William. He joined the R.A.F. in 1936 and his first posting was to 1 Squadron flying Hawker Furies. He stayed with the squadron, which converted to Hurricanes, and first saw action over France in the Spring of 1940 where he was shot down and wounded on the fourth day of the German blitzkrieg. Recovering from his wounds he instructed before a brief posting to 213 Squadron during which he volunteered for 421 Flight. The newly formed unit undertook dangerous operations including reconnaissance of German bomber formations heading for England over the Channel. As a Squadron Leader he was then sent to West Africa to command 128 Squadron. 1942 saw him commanding the famous 112 (Shark) Squadron in North Africa, in action right through the El Alamein campaign. He was posted to Malta as Wing Commander and back in the UK he flew Typhoons in the lead up to D-Day. With Pete Brothers he was sent to the USA to attend the US Staff School at Fort Leavenworth before joining Eisenhower's staff in the last months of the war. Post-war he continued in the R.A.F. serving around the world until his final posting as Group Captain RAF Chivenor. Billy retired in 1963 and went to Portugal where he ran a Bar and dealt in Real Estate before returning to live in Devon. In his flying career he accounted for more than 24 enemy aircraft. Billy Drake passed away in August 2011.

Group Captain John Gard'ner MiD

John Gard'ner was born in Dunedin, New Zealand, in 1918 and paid for his first flight while still at school. Learning to fly he set sail for England in 1938, one of the first group of New Zealanders to volunteer for the RAF. After training he was posted to 141 Squadron, at that time flying Blenheims but soon to convert to the brand new Boulton Paul Defiant. In early July 1940 the squadron was sent south to help with convoy patrols over the Channel. On 19 July 141 took off from Hawkinge, near the Kent coast, but were set upon by a mass of Me109s and the Defiants never stood a chance. John was shot down and recuperated in hospital, one of the lucky few to survive the slaughter. He eventually returned to his squadron and flew as a night fighter pilot on Defiants again and subsequently on Beaufighters and Mosquitos. After the war he flew Meteors before being seconded to the US Marine Corps where he flew Meteors and then Douglas F3D Skynight fighters. Having travelled at the age of 92 to be in England for the 70th anniversary of the Battle of Britain, John died in May 2011

Group Captain Allan Wright DFC*, AFC

Allan Wright was born in 1920 in Devon and entered Cranwell as a cadet in 1938. His first posting was to 92 Squadron, then at Tangmere, on Blenheims. However soon after they converted to Spitfires and Allan flew his first combat operations over Dunkirk in May 1940. Later, when the squadron was based at Biggin Hill, he saw some of the most intense fighting of the whole Battle of Britain. Force landing his Spitfire after combat on 30 September Allan was slightly wounded but returned and stayed with the squadron through until the Summer of 1941. Allan instructed for almost two years before converting to Beaufighters and joining 29 Squadron. After the war Allan took on various planning roles before becoming OC flying at Waterbeach with four squadrons of front line fighters including Hunters and Javelins. His final appointment was commanding the giant 'Golf balls', the Ballistic Missile Early Warning Station at Fylingdales on the Yorkshire coast. He died September 16 2015.

Flight Lieutenant Hazel Gregory

Hazel Gregory was born in 1922 and was living in Paris in early 1940. She returned to England as her mother was ill and, as France had fallen by the time her mother had recovered, she joined the WAAF. She became a plotter at the Headquarters of 11 Group, Fighter Command, at Uxbridge and served there right through the Battle of Britain. She was on duty on 15 September, perhaps the most important day of the battle, and well remembered Winston Churchill, who nicknamed her 'Coppertop', in the Operations room that day. She was commissioned in 1941 and sent to work at the top secret Bletchley Park facility as a code breaker. After two years she was promoted and posted to the Air Ministry as personal assistant to the Director of Intelligence. She worked there during the planning for the D-Day landings and regularly took minutes at top level meetings. Later in 1944 Hazel was posted to the Middle East where she married her fiancee and subsequently left the WAAF. Hazel retired in Lincolnshire where she lived until she passed away in 2012

Acknowledgements

We would like to thank many people involved in the creation of the interviews and this book. First of all there is Mike Lepine who has delivered a terrific script which complements the interviews perfectly. Then there is Darren Grice who seems to be able to transfer pages of words into a terrific design. Suzanne Gard'ner, for her encouragement and support of this project and Les Whitehouse of the Boulton Paul Association, Gary Rushbrooke, Steve Gleeson from the Battle of Britain Historical Society, Group Captain Patrick Tootal from the Battle of Britain Fighter Association, Colin Hudson and Caroline Fowler from Aces High Gallery in Wendover who have all been instrumental in contacting pilots for us in the past. And finally, the men themselves who gave freely of their time and memories and created an everlasting impression to us of men in battle.

Because these are personal accounts rather than cold histories, what and why certain events and details are recalled more vividly than others is down to how those individuals regarded them. The accounts are about what mattered to them.

All the accounts have been taken from filmed interviews which have then been transcribed and edited. Wherever possible the historical accuracy of the accounts has been checked but it may be that the passage of time means that some names, places or times are inaccurate.

Colin Higgs and Bruce Vigar

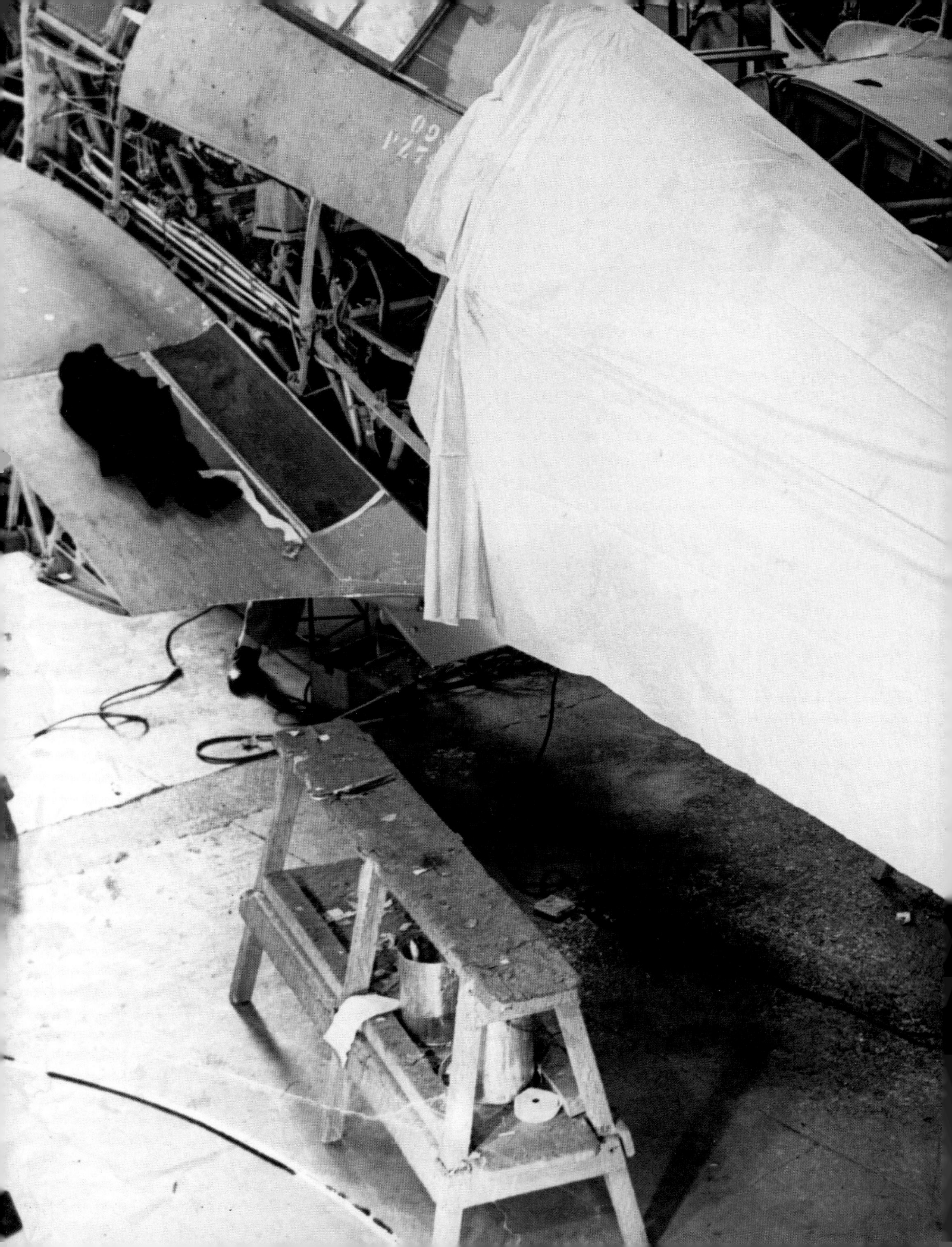